IN THEIR FOOTSTEPS

Qafa Family: Three Hundred Years of War

LOUIS ROMANO

© Copyright 2022 LOUIS ROMANO

All right reserved. No part of this book may be reproduced in any form or by any electronic or mechanical means, including information storage and retrieval system, without permission in writing from the publisher, except by a reviewer who may quote a brief passage in a review. Printed in the United States

ISBN: 979-8-3484-4124-1

Cover design by ALISON LORENZ
Photos: Qafa Family
Formatting: Spaaij Design

Dedicated by Simon Qafa to his parents.

Other books in the Heritage collection:

CARUSI: THE SHAME OF SICILY

True Crime books by Louis Romano:

TRUST AND BETRAYAL
BORN IN THE LIFE
JOHN ALITE MAFIA INTERNATIONAL

Fiction Books by Louis Romano:

Detective Vic Gonnella Series:
INTERCESSION
JUSTIFIED
YOU THINK I'M DEAD
THE BUTCHER OF PUNTA CANA
THE PIPELINE
SHANDA
THE SURGEON

Gino Ranno Mafia Series:
BESA
FISH FARM
GAME OF PAWNS
EXCLUSION

Young Adults:
ZIP CODE

Short Story & Poetry Series
ANXIETY'S NEST ANXIETY'S CURE
BEFORE I DROP DEAD

BEFORE I DROP DEAD: SHORT STORIES

CHAPTER ONE

DECEMBER 5, 1977

DETROIT, MICHIGAN

In a very modest home on Dane Street, a middle-class Detroit neighborhood, Pjeter and Liza Qafa raised their three sons and three daughters the best they could. The Albanian couple wanted their children to become Americans in every sense of the word and embrace the American way of life.

The Qafa family had immigrated to the United States to escape the suffocating, pathetic scourge of a life under communism in Albania.

Pjeter and Liza taught their children respect for the old Albanian ways of family devotion and the rules of the Kanun of Leke Dukagjini, devotion to the Roman Catholic Church, loyalty to their new adopted country, and a fervent disdain for communist rule. The Kanun, a compilation of northern Albanian traditional customary laws codified from oral history by a medieval prince, was a large part of the family's way of life.

It was the communist Albanian government that forced the Qafa family to flee the country which owned, or at least to attempt to own their very hearts and souls.

Like the Ottomans and the Serbs before them, it was communism that slaughtered so many of their friends and family. The very thought of the word communism evoked a hatred that was impossible to stifle. No political regime was able to successfully repress the Illyrian people over time. Not the Roman Empire, not the Byzantine Empire, not the Ottoman Empire, and certainly not these communists.

In their four-bedroom home in Detroit the boys, Nikola and Simon each had their own bedrooms. Kujtim, the first-born son, shared a bedroom with his own family on the second floor of the gray and white clapboard home. The three Qafa sisters shared two other upstairs rooms while the parents' bedroom was on the first level near the almost always busy, small, and immaculate kitchen.

Simon recalls a four o'clock in the morning telephone call which changed his and his family's lives forever. And not for the better.

Simon was awoken by the sharp ringing of the only telephone in their home—a black wall phone in the tidy downstairs kitchen. He heard his father's heavy steps as Pjeter Qafa walked from his bedroom to answer the call.

Like it happened just yesterday, Simon remembers the terrifying muffled words he heard his father say.

"Today? In the street? Is he dead? Who shot him? Have the shooters been caught?"

Moments later, Simon's father slowly walked up the creaky, wooden stairs to awaken his sons with the terrible news.

Pjeter Qafa's kumar, his best friend with whom he had fought side-by-side within the Albanian mountains against the communists, and who he'd saved from a certain death years ago, was shot dead in New York City. Both men were fearless anti-communist guerillas in the villages, hills, and mountains of Albania.

Pjeter's kumar, Gjon Gjinaj was shot by two unknown assailants at 12:30 a.m. that morning where he was working as a doorman in a swanky building on Park Avenue and 77th Street in New York City.

Gjon Gjinaj was a handsome, vibrant, young sixty-two-year-old man with a full head of salt-and-pepper hair, who, along with Pjeter Qafa, had worked tirelessly alongside each other to overthrow the communist Albanian government.

Gjon had worked closely with MI 6 and CIA operatives to do whatever necessary to topple the government and restore democracy for his beloved country and its people.

It eventually cost him his life on the concrete pavement in Manhattan.

Factions in the communist Yugoslavian and Albanian governments wanted to eliminate any threat to their power, which included Pjeter and his beloved kumar. Gjon Gjinaj was the easier, more visible target to be taken first. It was a paid hit on Gjinaj. Pjeter's time at the end of a paid for communist gun would come soon enough.

Liza Qafa had made coffee for her husband and their sons before dawn that terrible morning. She also left a bottle of homemade raki, should Pjeter want to fortify himself from the awful news. The aroma of something delicious being baked in Liza's kitchen was hardly noticed by the grieving family.

With his sons sitting around the white and silver Formica kitchen table, Pjeter Qafa declared that he would, in the Albanian tradition from the pages of the Kanun, take responsibility for the family and go to New York to avenge the death of his dearest friend. The Kanun was specific about blood revenge, Gjakmarrja. To Pjeter, his kumar was as good as his own blood and therefore needed to be avenged. No money, property, or anything other than blood would avenge this heinous killing.

Simon Qafa sat quiet for a few minutes before he spoke with authority, "Baba, you are not able to go. Your health is not good, and your English is worse. Kujtim, (the eldest son whose godfather was Gjon Gjinaj) has three little children who need him, and Nikola is too young. This responsibility falls upon me. I will go to New York and avenge our kumar's killing."

It made absolute sense to Pjeter Qafa, and so it was.

Simon was only twenty-three years old and awaiting his American citizenship papers to be finalized. He was also about to fulfill a life-long dream and sign a one-year contract to play professional soccer with the Detroit Express of the North American

Soccer League. Jimmy Hill himself, the owner of the Detroit Express, had offered the position to Simon and had invited him to practice with the famed United Coventry team in the United Kingdom. This was an absolute honor that was not offered to many players. Simon was one of the best prospects the team had, and the future looked extremely bright for his athletic career.

An article in the Detroit Free Press had just announced the signing of Simon Qafa to the BESA team.

"Before the start of the season, Detroit Besa signed Mladen Tomasevic, a twenty-three-year-old Yugoslavian second division player. Forward Simon Qafa was a former New York Eagles player. During the season defender, Alex Dreshaj was sold to Detroit Express in the American Soccer League."

Simon Qafa's dream of becoming a professional soccer player would soon be realized. But first and foremost, he had to do his duty as an Albanian male for the honor of his family.

All Simon had to do now was go to New York, find out who was behind the killing of his father's kumar, kill whoever was responsible, and return to Detroit.

None of this was an easy task for a young man who, not long ago, was in the seminary in Rome studying to become a Catholic priest.

Bardh Bisaku, Simon's friend and partner in some business dealings, loaned his 1977 Silver Cadillac Eldorado for Qafa's trip to New York. (Bardh would be killed a few years later, in 1981, in the Holiday Inn in New City, New York, with suspicions of involvement in the drug trade.)

Simon's first trip to New York on his self-appointed mission of revenge was strictly for reconnaissance.

Simon took the long, eleven-hour drive alone. His mind raced with images of how he was going to meet up with various anti-communist freedom fighters who were close to his father and what he would do when he saw them. He pictured himself eventually killing the shooters and escaping back home to Detroit to fulfill his dreams to be a professional athlete.

Pjeter Qafa had provided Simon with various names of trusted New York Albanians whom he could contact on his behalf to help with his plan of revenge. These friends would guide Simon toward information on the killer or the men who ordered the assassination.

Simon checked into a hotel, which was owned by a friend of his, near Manhattan, in Yonkers, New York. This hotel room would be his base of operations during his visit.

Day by day, Simon was able to glean the information he needed from trusted sources.

Aside from discovering who was responsible for the kumar's murder, paramount in Simon's mind was the danger his own father was in. Everyone he spoke with in New York told Simon that the word was out. It was clear Pjeter Qafa was next to be murdered by the same communist sympathizers who had killed the kumar. It was simply a matter of time. Simon's father could be kicked at any time.

Without hesitation, and perhaps with the impetuous emotions of a young man, Simon called the Albanian Consulate in New York City. In other words, it seemed as if Simon had completely lost his mind.

"To protect my father and the rest of my family, I let it be known, if one more freedom fighter is killed, I, Simon Qafa, will blow up the entire consulate and everyone in it," Simon stated.

The embassy took Simon's threat seriously and quickly obtained an order of protection against Simon Qafa, prohibiting him from being within one hundred yards of the consulate. This would not play well on the Kosovo-born Qafa in his quest to be granted his United States citizenship.

As things developed, none of Simon's father's contacts knew who had actually performed the shooting of their kumar, but it was crystal clear who ordered the shooting. That information would be more than sufficient to take out the blood revenge.

Two known communist sympathizers, who took their orders—as well as money—from the communist Albanian government, were identified by Qafa family friends as the conspirators who'd ordered the murder of Gjon Gjinaj. These men were proud of their involvement and, like most political fanatics, could not keep their participation quiet.

Simon, armed with this information, returned to Detroit to plan the assassination of two brothers, Zef and Gjok. (The names have been changed to protect the fine families that are still active in the Albanian community in the United States.)

Pjeter Qafa gave Simon his blessing, and the hit on the two brothers in New York was developed in great detail.

With tears in his eyes, Pjeter Qafa kissed his son and sent him on his way with the hope and prayers that God would protect him.

Simon returned once again to New York in the borrowed Cadillac which now also transported a clean, unregistered German STG 44 automatic machine gun. This powerful and deadly machine gun, known as a Sturmgewehr, cost Simon $2,000 in 1977, almost the price of a new car. Simon also carried a Smith and Wesson .38 S six-shot revolver handgun.

The eleven-hour drive gave Simon plenty of time to plot his revenge, mulling his plan over and over in his mind's eye. The excitement built the closer he got to New York. He could almost feel his blood pressure mounting as the Cadillac's odometer ticked off the miles.

"There is a big difference between planning a shooting in your mind, scene by scene, and actually shooting two human beings when the adrenaline is flowing, and the heart is pounding. Some men will lose their nerve the very second, they are faced with their human target," Simon stated. The moment of truth would soon be at hand.

Through the close-knit Albanian grapevine, Zef and Gjok knew that Pjeter Qafa's son was in New York and were rightfully afraid for their safety. They were holed up in their house on Powers Street in the crowded working-class Williamsburg section of Brooklyn.

Simon recalled, "I received a call at three o'clock that afternoon telling me the brothers would be leaving their home that evening to attend an event. I think it may have been a wake, but I don't remember that detail anymore. I do remember, however, how the adrenaline began to surge throughout my body. Butterflies filled my stomach. I immediately loaded my two guns and quickly checked out of the Holiday Inn in Yonkers and headed for Brooklyn. I was very nervous. I had two goals. To shoot them dead without hesitation, and to get away cleanly and immediately drive back to Detroit."

After finding the Powers Street house where the brothers lived, Simon parked his car around the corner and waited for his opportunity, while also trying to keep his heart rate and his hands steady. After all, Simon was not a killer by any stretch of the imagination.

The porch light on the front of the small house was not lit—likely intentionally so as not to give anyone a clear vision to shoot the brothers. The interior of the house was dimly lit.

It was barely a week before Christmas. The weather was quite cold, and it was already dark outside. Simon walked around the neighborhood and noticed the block on Powers Street and the surrounding area was filled with people walking about, shopping, getting home from work, and visiting friends. He opted not to use the powerful Sturmgewehr so as not to harm any innocent bystanders. Simon figured the handgun would be a much more controllable and practical weapon, so he tucked it under his black jacket and into the belt around his waist. He didn't have gloves, and his hands had gotten cold. He left his hands in his coat pockets, occasionally blowing on them to keep the tingling from turning his fingers numb and affecting his accuracy.

Just around seven o'clock that evening, the brothers left their one family house and walked down Powers Street just as Simon had been advised.

Simon crossed to the other side of the street where the targets were briskly walking. Nervously aware of their surroundings, the brothers walked to the opposite side of the street where Simon had come from. They both looked behind several times to see if they were being followed. Simon quickly crossed back over to the side of the street where the brothers walked. At that moment, the brothers realized they were in deadly trouble. They'd spotted their executioner.

Simon could hear the blood beating in his ears as he quickly raised the pistol in front of him. One of the brothers was tall, the other quite a bit shorter, and Simon aimed his pistol from about forty feet away. The brothers froze in their footsteps. Simon Qafa squeezed off five shots from the .38, hitting both brothers, who fell quickly to the gray, concrete pavement. The brothers lay quietly on the ground in two heaps. After the popping shots, the street went deadly silent for a moment. Everything was moving in slow motion. Simon could not see the damage that was done and had no idea of the severity of the men's wounds.

Qafa held the handgun down by his side and rapidly, without running, made his way back toward the parked Cadillac, tucking the pistol back into his waistband.

As he approached the car, without warning, a small army of plainclothes detectives and uniformed police in unmarked cars surrounded Simon with guns drawn, screaming all kinds of obscenities and commands.

Unbeknownst to the young shooter, the police had shut down the entrance to the Williamsburg Bridge, and Metropolitan Avenue was cordoned off which would have been his escape route to Manhattan or Queens respectively.

From there, he would have made his way home to Detroit.

Simon Qafa was immediately thrown to the ground, arrested, and put into handcuffs.

Simon Qafa had been set up.

CHAPTER TWO

For over three-hundred years, the Qafa family name has been synonymous with fighting for Albanian independence. Since the 1600's, Qafa men have lost their lives and taken lives fighting against the Ottoman Turks, the Yugoslavian Serbs, or the communists.

In his book, ZANË I TË PARVE TË MI, the late Dedë Qafa tells the history of the Qafa family from 1637 in their ancestral town of Fushë Arrëz, Albania. Dedë Qafa was a cousin of Simon Qafa. He researched records on the family as well as descriptive oral history that spanned over three hundred years.

In antiquity, the Qafas were one of five families belonging to the Spaqi tribe in Mirdita. The Qafa family flag was the same for all Mirdita tribes with a white background and a fir tree branch. The fir tree was added by the Qafa family to distinguish it from the rest of Mirdita. A person carrying that flag, or even a tree branch on their clothing, guaranteed safe passage throughout the region. The Qafa men were known for their ferocious revenge should any of their tribe be harmed during a period where bandits were prominent in Albania.

Going back to the mid 1600's, the family tree of Qafa men illustrates the bravery, fearlessness, ferocity, and loyalty. The Qafa men had warlike attitudes imprinted upon their personalities.

Laska and his son Gjergi fought the Ottoman Turks. After these brave men, Mark Qafa fought gallantly against the Serbs, then his son Prenk (Simon Qafa's grandfather) was killed in action against the Serbs, followed by his son, Çupi Qafa, who lost his life in 1916, also battling the Serbs.

Pjeter Çup Qafa took up arms against the communists and became legend in modern Albanian history.

In the late 1600's the Qafas were the first family to start commerce in Mirdita. Throughout the region, the Qafa family sold and distributed meat, wool, and grease, which was made from the plentiful fir trees.

Ever industrious, the Qafas opened a *hani*, which was akin to the modern bed and breakfast lodge to accommodate travelers and other merchants.

Generation after generation of Qafa family men and women did what was necessary to feed their families and protect them from the enemies of their times.

In 1916 in the Albanian region of Mirdita, in the tiny mountain town of Fushë Arrëz, Pjeter Çup Qafa was born. Çup (pronounced Chup in English) was to designate the son of the murdered Çup Qafa.

The Yugoslavian government had dispatched a battalion of Serbian soldiers to Mirdita with strict orders to burn the churches, massacre anyone who resisted, and otherwise terrorize and control the population. Spilling Albanian blood was an absolute pleasure for the brutal Serbian soldiers.

Another Qafa, a ferocious fighter Nrec Nue Qafa known in the region as the "Serbs worst nightmare" got word that the Serbs were going to pass by Fushë-Arrëz to reach Kuksi and then proceed back to Serbia. Nrec summoned his brother Zef and his cousins Çup and Pjeter Qafa as well as other friends from Fushë-Arrëz preparing them to lay in wait on both sides of the road. Then men all hid in the bushes and behind trees. When the Serbs arrived dancing and singing Nrec Nue Qafa opened fire signaling all the men to join in. Within three hours the entire Serb platoon was massacred. Only Çup Qafa was killed from the Qafa clan.

Pjeter Qafa's father, Çup, was killed on Christmas Eve, the night before Pjeter was born. Pjeter Qafa was predestined to become a freedom fighter, but this time against another incipient enemy—communism.

The Qafa family now consisted only of Pjeter Qafa's mother and his only brother, Prenush. They lived in abject poverty, like most citizens in the region. They struggled to avoid starvation, living the best they could off the small parcel of mountainous land Çup Qafa had left behind for his two sons.

Time passed, and at only twenty-three years old, Pjeter was the head of the Gojan wood mill in Mirdita, working tirelessly to put a meager amount of food on the table for his family. Working at the wood mill was considered a good job at the time.

Photographs of Pjeter Qafa show a powerfully built young man who was not particularly tall. However, his intense look was dominated by large, piercing, dark, almost doe-like eyes, a trimmed moustache, short dark hair, and black bushy eyebrows, making him a visual force to be reckoned with.

Sadly, at twenty-three years old, Pjeter's brother Prenush was killed fighting bravely for the anti-King Zog faction of the Mirdita militia. Another Qafa family casualty.

At the end of World War II, an even more impoverished Albania was sent into a further downward economic spiral under the yoke of communism.

In 1946, the Mirdita Prince Kapitan Mark Gjonmarkaj, an avid anti-communist and head of all the Mirdita tribes, declared war on the communist government. His goal was a total overthrow of the current system and a return to democracy.

Pjeter Qafa immediately joined the underground movement to fight the Albanian government for the same goals as Gjonmarkaj. Freedom for all Albanians was the ultimate and elusive goal.

Tragically, Kapitan Mark Gjonmarkaj was killed soon after he started the rebellion in 1946. Pjeter Qafa, along with a band of other guerilla fighters, took to the mountains of Mirdita as many of their ancestors had done before them. Fighting seemed to have been printed in Pjeter's DNA and in his soul.

The fearless Pjeter Qafa and his loyal group fought long and hard, living off the land with help from local peasants, who provided them with cheese, raw onions, dried meat, and some raki to sustain them during their daily shooting and bombing battles against government troops.

The army had strict orders to capture or kill the small guerilla group using whatever means possible. To be captured by the communists would have been far worse than death.

Sadly, in 1949, the freedom fighters succumbed to defeat against the overpowering communist troops. This unthinkable loss forced Pjeter, his wife, and small daughter Dava—along with a band of fifty-one others from the Mirdita group of guerillas—to flee to the safety of nearby Kosovo. They were intensely pursued by government forces with one objective—to kill them all.

Life on the run was incredibly difficult. With an average elevation of 708 meters above sea level, Albania is
one of the most mountainous countries in the world. The rocky and rugged terrain covers more than seventy percent of Albania's total territory. Mountain peaks reaching heights of more than 6,600 feet with few paved or dirt roads to help in their escape on foot toward Kosovo made life miserable at best. Danger was a constant. The sense of fear was palpable.

Armed with pistols, knives, rifles, machine guns, hand-carried grenades, and homemade bombs, the Mirdita group hid from the communists in mountain caves during daylight hours and traveled under the darkness of night.

Mountain summits zig-zagged the horizon as far as the eye could see. Peaks with shades of light and dark gray rock, dotted by patches of evergreen trees and hard scrabble bushes, made the views nothing less than spectacular. Caves—more than anyone could count—were the natural hiding places for the freedom fighters and the bane of the pursuing army's existence.

One night, while the group from Mirdita was fleeing from a group of soldiers, Pjeter and Liza's young daughter, Dava, would not stop crying. Pjeter Qafa knew that the child's incessant sobbing would attract the pursuing soldiers, putting the entire group of Mirdita freedom fighters in peril. Nothing could stop the child from crying.

Pjeter, as leader of the guerillas, instructed his wife in all seriousness to, "Throw her in the river, or we will all be killed."

"I would rather die myself than kill my daughter," his weeping wife, Liza, replied.

Pjeter Qafa, undeterred by his wife's pleading, lunged for the child to throw her in the river himself, only to be thwarted by two members of the group who took turns carrying the wailing child and soothing her discomfort, likely caused by the inclement weather. They all narrowly escaped sure death. Pjeter put the lives of his fellow patriots in front of his own daughter, his own blood.

***

Kosovo was the freedom fighters only hope for survival from the pursuing horde of communist soldiers. The Geneva Convention supported anyone fleeing from a communist-bloc country to take political refuge in Kosovo.

Even in the face of the Geneva Convention, the Yugoslavian government persisted in their attempt to neutralize the ethnic Albanians, displacing them every three years, spreading the families throughout Kosovo. The Albanians were constantly prevented from assimilating and planting roots.

In December of 1950, while Pjeter Qafa was living in exile in Kosovo, another renowned anti-communist freedom fighter, and Pjeter's future kumar, Gjon Gjinaj, had parachuted under cover of darkness into Albania. Qafa and Gjinaj did not know of each other well, only meeting once very briefly.

There was a time when the two rebels had crossed paths. In 1939, in the home of a Catholic priest for a meeting of anti-communists, Pjeter Qafa sang two patriotic melodies to the small assembly. These songs would later inexplicably save Pjeter's life.

Gjon Gjinaj's parachute was noticed by the pursuing army, and he was set upon and attacked by a squad of communist Albanian soldiers. Five serious wounds threatened his life, but he was saved and taken— literally carried—by Guerilla Fichteri and was hidden in caves within the vast Munella Mountain range.

The Kapedani of Mirdita, Gjon Marka Gjoni, head of the Albanian anti-communist organization based in Rome, Italy, was constantly monitoring the conditions of their fellow rebels in Albania. Information on the condition of Gjon Gjinaj came to the Kapedani from United States CIA and Great Britain MI 6 operatives determined to disrupt the communist government of Tirana, the Albanian capital.

Pjeter Qafa received communication from the head of the Kapedani, Gjon Marka Gjoni.

"You are to go into Albania, to the Munella mountain zone where you will meet with our friends. They will escort you to one Gjon Gjinaj who is badly wounded, and you will return Gjinaj safely to Kosovo."

Pjeter Qafa, without questioning his superiors' orders, left Kosovo immediately, leaving his family behind in favor of his duty to the cause. He once again crossed the border illegally and at great personal risk, back into the land of his ancestors.

A Jeep was dispatched to bring Pjeter from where he was living in Kosovo to the Albanian border. After that, he was on his own.

Walking through the rugged, mountainous terrain of Albania for three days, under the cover of darkness, Pjeter Qafa met his fellow freedom fighters as designed, who escorted him to the cave in the Munella mountains where the injured Gjon Gjinaj was suffering greatly from his battle wounds.

The weather averaged forty-five degrees Fahrenheit during the night, which was cold but bearable. However, in December, rain in Albania is almost a certainty. The nights that it rained made walking and climbing extremely difficult and hazardous due to mud and flooding.

Pjeter ignored the rain, keeping his mind focused on reaching the injured compatriot and completing his assignment.

Pjeter helped to clean and redress Gjon Gjinaj's wounds, and after a day of rest, he carried the injured compatriot at night on his back for nearly five days, back to the Kosovo border and temporary freedom.

Traveling only at night was treacherous in pitch blackness, but the daylight would have been far too dangerous. Once the army learned of Pjeter Qafa's presence in the area, the two men were being tirelessly sought

after by the communist army, who added more men to the search. To capture, torture, and ultimately execute Pjeter Qafa and Gjon Gjinaj would be a coup for the local comandante and a major victory for the government in Tirana.

Kapedani had already lost two sons to the communists, and two of his sons had escaped to Italy. After Pjeter returned him to Kosovo, after a period of recouperation, Gjinaj, years later eventually made his way to Germany, out of harm's way. Qafa and Gjinaj bonded as brothers in the caves and mountains.

***

Like many other patriots, Pjeter Qafa crossed the border from Kosovo to Albania countless times. His sojourns were made to save his fellow guerillas' lives, to attack the vicious Albanian forces, and continue to take orders from the Kapedani in Rome via the CIA and MI 6.

In his later years, Pjeter had told the following story to his children and grandchildren many times.

Later in 1951, doing reconnaissance in the Albanian mountains, Pjeter Qafa, seeking food and refuge from severe weather, had come to a small house. When he approached the tattered dwelling, several men, brandishing rifles, came upon, him ready to shoot him dead.

"I said, 'hey you idiots, I'm Pjeter Çup Qafa. Put the guns down,'" Qafa would recall.

Not knowing Pjeter by sight and thinking it was a typical communist trick, the men all leveled their rifles and handguns at Pjeter.

Suddenly a man's voice came from inside the house.

"Wait one second. Don't shoot him yet. If he is truly Pjeter Çup Qafa, ask him what song he sang in 1939 at the priest's home?"

Pjeter Çup Qafa yelled out the name of both songs he had sung back in 1939.

"It is truly him. Open the door," Gjon Gjinaj ordered. They embraced each other and drank raki into the early morning. That brief meeting at the priest's home had unwittingly saved Pjeter's life.

In his incredibly detailed eyewitness book, *One Man's Journey to Freedom: Escape From the Iron Curtain,* Gene Kortsha details the destruction of his country by communism. Kortsha tells a story of meeting with Pjeter Çup Qafa in October,1952.

Pjeter and two of his associates, Hila Shilaku and Deda Mehilli, were disguised as Albanian Sigurami, the secret police from their shoes to their caps, complete with German Mauser rifles.

Gene Kortsha writes, "It was exhilarating to see armed anti-communists. In Albania, firearms were the symbol of manhood. In communist Albania at that time, only the communists had firearms."

Pjeter and his associates were tangible proof that things in Albania did not need to be the way they were.

Kortsha decided to take Pjeter into his confidence. "Pjeter, I want to ask a big favor of you. If we are ever surrounded, I want your word of honor that you will shoot me before you kill yourself," Kortsha implored.

Pjeter looked at Kortsha and asked, "Do you have a weapon?" Kortsha replied that he did not, indeed, have a gun of any kind.

Kortsha continued, "Before I knew what he was doing, Pjeter Qafa pulled a revolver out of his belt and handed it to me. He reached into his pocket and gave me a hand grenade. It was an Italian aluminum hand grenade intended to make a lot of smoke and noise to allow the user to escape in the confusion. The revolver was something else. It was a Nagant, originally made in Belgium; it was a beautiful weapon ... it was the favorite gun of political assassins. Under the circumstances, it was also the best guarantee that the communists would not catch me alive."

Kortsha told Pjeter Qafa, "Pjeter, I cannot accept it. You must not endanger your safety because of me." Pjeter's bushy dark eyebrows (a Qafa trait) went up, and he again displayed that renown friendly smile.

"Keep it, and don't worry," Pjeter replied.

"Years later, in Detroit, I asked Pjeter why he had given me his handgun," Kortsha recalled.

Pjeter Qafa, in his inimitable way, replied, "I could see the anxious expression in your eyes. It was obvious that you had suffered much. So, I decided instead of me taking your life, I would give you my gun and let you do it yourself."

This, in and of itself, illustrates the leadership and sage advice that helped to make Pjeter Qafa a legend in the mountains.

***

Pjeter put his own life in danger many times. He became a legend among the people of Albania and Kosovo. He fought fearlessly and passionately, bringing over one hundred wounded or stranded guerilla fighters to safety from Albania across the closely watched

Kosovo border. Qafa was—like many of the men he helped escape the communists—sentenced to death in absentia. If they were captured, after being mercilessly tortured for information on the freedom fighters, they would have been summarily executed. Death would have been a welcomed relief.

Another legendary story of Pjeter Qafa was verified by men within his circle of freedom fighters.

In 1954, Enver Hoxha, the powerful Albanian communist revolutionary and politician, had already been the twenty-second Prime Minister of Albania for the last ten years.

Hoxha, in an attempt to bait Qafa, declared, "Pjeter Qafa can roam around the mountains of Mirdita and hide in the caves all he wants, but he doesn't have the balls to come to Tirana."

At that time, the *Drejtoria e Sigurimit të Shtetit*,

commonly called the *Sigurimi*, was the dreaded state security, intelligence, and secret police service of the People's Socialist Republic of Albania.

To protect Albania from external danger was the official responsibility of the Sigurimi.

In reality, the main objective was to suppress political activity within the population and hold the existing political system in power. They were akin to the Nazi SS.

The primary mission of the Sigurimi was to destroy any attempted counterrevolutions, such as Pjeter Qafa's group of freedom fighters, and to

suppress any and all opposition to the existing political system.

The Sigurimi were very effective in their activities and were not at all interested in crimes from one person to another. They did not act as a local police force. Their job was to destroy any threat against Hoxha's regime. It is said that every third citizen in Albania was either interrogated or spent time in labor camps due to the effectiveness of the ruthless Sigurimi.

The Sigurimi and Enver Hoxha knew that the challenge the Prime Minister had put out to Pjeter Qafa could likely entrap the fearless Qafa's ego.

Donning an Albanian general's uniform (the Albanian and Yugoslavian uniforms were virtually identical at that time) Pjeter Qafa, with his chest out and his head held high under his decorated hat, walked into the famed Hotel Dajti near Rinia Park in downtown Tirana. At that time, the Dajti was the main meeting place for international visitors and diplomats and was monitored every minute of the day by the Sigurimi. Every room in the hotel was bugged with microphones, listened in on by an entire staff in the sub-basement of the hotel.

Pjeter Qafa, sat for a while at a table in the restaurant, had several cups of coffee, and ate a full breakfast under the noses of the Sigurimi.

When he was done with his meal, Pjeter asked the waiter for a pen and sheet of paper. He left the following note on the table:

"I am Pjeter Çup Qafa who comes to Tirana to have my breakfast, and there isn't a fucking thing you can do about it. I will return whenever I want."

Upon seeing the note, the waiter ran to a known Sigurimi agent who was sitting in the lobby of the hotel, handing him Qafa's note.

At that moment, all hell broke loose. Pjeter had fled. All over Tirana, roadblocks were set up to find Qafa, with the police and every available Sigurimi scouring the city for the daring freedom fighter. They never captured the cunning Pjeter.

***

There could be no doubt that when Gjon Gjinaj was murdered in cold blood in Manhattan in 1977 that the Qafa family would seek their ancient blood Gjakmarrja. It was Simon Qafa, the son of Pjeter, who would take the vengeance. Blood had to be taken.

***

Pjeter Çup Qafa had decided to go to a traditional feast organized by a friend of his in the town of Puka, a communist stronghold.

Pjeter left the relative safety of Kosovo and the protection of the mountains to attend the feast and see old friends. This risky effort nearly cost Pjeter his life.

After hearing word of his planned attendance, the Sigurimi pulled out all the stops to capture Pjeter Qafa.

One of the Sigurimi top agents at that time was Mark Dodani, whose only job was to capture Pjeter Qafa alive and return him to their unique form of torture and justice in Tirana. Dodani set his trap.

Dodani had ten agents assigned to him by the Albanian government with the strictest of orders to capture their arch nemesis.

After the feast ended, Pjeter Qafa, with a full belly and a full head from the raki, made his way back to the qualified security of the mountains to begin his return journey to his family in Kosovo.

It was after midnight, and the moon shone its light along a narrow, dirt walking path in the town of Miliska in the Puka mountains. No cars could possibly navigate this path, only horses could be used to traverse the area. This dirt path was the only viable way out of the area. One side of the path had steep hills with dense brush, while the other had a more than one-hundred-foot drop into a ravine.

Dodani ordered his men to split into two groups, five and five, giving them specific instructions to let Pjeter Qafa pass by so they could entrap him.

Pjeter unwittingly passed the hidden five heavily

armed agents and walked directly into the sight of Mark Dodani and his other five men.

Dodani shouted at the unsuspecting Qafa, "Pjeter Qafa, drop your weapon. I am here to take you alive, but we will shoot you dead if need be. You are covered on both sides. I order you to surrender now!"

Without a word, Pjeter knew what he had to do. He could not out-shoot the ten men and their commander on the path, so he instantly dove off the dirt path down the steep ravine.

Pjeter instinctively let his body go limp as he bounced off the rocks on the way down to the ravine. He knew his odds of being severely injured or killed were high, and he remembered his oath never to be taken alive by the communists. As he fell, he tucked his machine gun close to his body, which took the brunt force of the rocks. The weapon likely saved him from breaking ribs and possible death.

Pjeter landed at the base of the hill with a minor split lip and a lot of dirt in his eyes and mouth, but otherwise alive.

Donadi's men scrambled to find and attack the fearless Qafa.

Dodani bellowed his commands, "What the hell are you all doing? Relax, we will take our time going down the
ravine. I don't need any of you injured. Anyway, after a fall like that, Qafa is probably dead."

The men heeded their commanders' words and found a slower and safer path, expecting to find Pjeter Qafa's battered, bloody body at the bottom.

As Dodani and his ten agents traversed the land and began descending, Pjeter Qafa had already wedged himself against a huge oak tree, pointing his firearm in the direction of his pursuers.

Qafa had the strategic advantage of his position against the men coming downhill. He also had good cover of the tree if need be. The moon had illuminated the hill to help Qafa if he decided to open fire.

Qafa fired one shot near the men.

"I am Pjeter Çup Qafa," he hollered. "No communist scum will ever take me alive. I swear that I will kill you all if you try to get closer. Tell Enver Hoxha, that communist pig, you failed at your duty. I promise you all one thing: If I ever catch any one of you again, I will kill you on the spot and then kill your entire family and anyone else who knows you."

To add strength to his words, Pjeter Qafa strafed the ground in front of the men with machine gun fire.

Knowing that discretion was the better part of valor and valuing his and his men's lives, Dodani ordered the agents to fall back. Qafa vanished into the night and to the safety of the mountains.

***

During a trip to Albania, after the fall of communism while visiting family and friends, Simon Qafa asked around about Mark Dodani among his many personal contacts. Simon wanted to set up a face-to-face meeting with an aged Sigurimi agent.

They met at the Hotel Tirana where Simon promised that Dodani would be safe.

Simon offered, "It was an incredible event to meet this man. The man who sought after my father on the orders of the communist government, but never succeeded. Dodani told me, 'Your father was like an eel. He would slip away right from under our noses. I respected him enormously. I actually had fond feelings for his determination and bravery while I chased him. Frankly, at times, I thought I would join Pjeter Qafa under different circumstances."

Near the end of their coffee meeting, Mark Dodani became very serious, very somber, almost melancholy. Dodani spoke softly, just above a whisper. "Simon, I must admit something to you, and I'm not ashamed to say these words. When I was told your father was back in Kosovo, coming from Detroit, I would go into hiding from him. I had heard that your father would enter Albania illegally with the purpose of looking for me. I was afraid he would hunt me down and kill me. Obviously, my hiding prevented me from being murdered. I must tell you that Pjeter Qafa had an intense look. A dangerous look not seen in many men. I see that same look in your eyes."

Dodani continued, "Simon, I will ask for your promise. I ask that Simon Qafa not ever go after my family to take revenge against them because of my history with Pjeter Qafa."

Simon replied, "Mark Dodani, I have no reason to come after you or your family. You were doing your job even though I disagree with your philosophy. I give you my promise; I will not go after you or your family. Understand one thing, however. If I find out who killed my cousin, Pal Qafa, whoever they are, they will surely die by my hand."

"You are so very much like your father. Not only in looks, but in your wise judgement. I thank you for your promise," Dodani said.

CHAPTER THREE

Lying in his lumpy bunk, in the chill and dampness of his blue and gray cell, alone and staring at the steel door that separated freedom from incarceration, Simon Qafa had plenty of time to reflect upon his twenty-four years. When the metallic sound of his cell's lock snapped for the first time, Qafa knew the rigors of conformity, monotony, and loneliness required of prison life would not play well for him. Leaving his loving, religious, and close-knit family, as well as his girlfriend, back in Detroit was enough to make the sinking feeling of confinement push him into despair.

Simon's home for the next three years would be the maximum-security Clinton Correctional Facility at Dannemora, in upstate New York.

Dannemora sits in a remote corner of New York State on a desolate, barren plain. Its thick, gray, stone walls encase the prison. In the summer, sweltering heat beats down until the walls which leak a sticky sweat. In the winter, the freezing Canadian winds coat the walls with thick layers if ice.

The prison was built in 1844. It took one hundred and seventy-one years before an escape was made. In 2015, two prisoners, Richard Matt and David Sweat, escaped by digging under the prison with the help of two prison employees. Matt was soon shot dead, and Sweat was shot and taken back into custody. New York State spent twenty-three million dollars to capture the escaped prisoners.

Escape was not something that entered Simon Qafa's mind. He would do his time and play the cards he was delt.

Along with nearly three thousand other inmates, one to a cell with forty-three prisoners to each cellblock, Simon Qafa immediately lamented his situation.

However, not once did he regret shooting the two men who had ordered the killing of his dear father Pjeter's kumar, Gjon Gjinaj. That was his duty deeply ingrained within his culture. Simon's biggest regret was getting caught.

If I would have used the damn machine gun, they would both have been dead, splattered all over the Brooklyn sidewalk, Simon thought. He was angry that his targets survived the five .38 Special projectiles he'd pumped into their flesh.

Simon was also quite relieved that he'd received a fairly light sentence for attempted homicide. Things could have been far worse if one or both of the communist sympathizer brothers were killed. Simon could have easily received thirty years to life prison sentence.

One of the brothers Simon had gunned down was shot in the upper leg, while the other was wounded in his lower chest and arm.

Qafa ran through the entire scenario over and over in

his mind. Who had set him up? Were the police staking out some other crime, or was it simply a coincidence that they were there? Was it the same people who informed him that his victims would be leaving their home the night of the shooting, or was it another rat, or group of rats, from the communist sympathizers in New York?

It was likely better off that he would never know the answers to these questions. It was bad enough that the males in the Qafa family—Simon's brothers and his elderly, unhealthy father—were now faced with a multi-year blood feud that put them all in deadly danger back in Detroit, or anywhere they traveled, for that matter.

After Simon was indicted and before his court date, several well-to-do families from Montenegro—out of respect for Simon's legendary freedom fighter father—had visited Pjeter Qafa's home in Detroit with bags. The bags were filled with cash to make sure Simon could post bail and get a lawyer who would help reduce a potentially long prison sentence.

Qafa could have easily received a sentence of ten to twenty years or more for attempted murder, save for the fact that the shooting was Simon's first felony offense and also because of the sage advice of his veteran trial judge, Lombardo, who had taken a personal liking to the young Albanian.

The Assistant District Attorney, Boyce, was seeking a ten- to fifteen-year sentence for Qafa. A plea deal was put on the table for seven years flat.

There was something about Simon Qafa that Judge Lombardo liked. Perhaps it was Qafa's early daily arrival at the courtroom where he and the judge would exchange pleasantries and chat before anyone else arrived. Lombardo saw for himself that the young man was not a true criminal, but a man who was fulfilling his cultural duty. Or perhaps the Sicilian-American judge somewhat understood family loyalty and the eye-for-an-eye vengeance that was required within the Albanian culture.

Lombardo was also fascinated and intrigued that only three years prior to the shooting, Simon Qafa had been studying for the priesthood in Vatican City. More on that later.

When Judge Lombardo passed Qafa's sentence at one point in the hearings, the judge opined, "Mr. Qafa, you are not a criminal in your heart. You are an honorable man. It is a sin that you are not sitting where I am right now because you certainly have the aptitude and the spirit."

Whatever the reason for Judge Lombardo's personal bias, the judge had privately encouraged the defense attorney not to accept the District Attorney's plea deal. Lombardo had already made up his mind to give the minimum sentence allowed by law to Simon Pjeter Qafa.

When Lombardo passed his lenient sentence and sounded his gavel, Simon Qafa was now the property of the Department of Corrections for the next three years of his life.

CHAPTER FOUR

Another story of the bravery and resolve of Pjeter Qafa took place in November of 1952.

While hiding in a mountain cave in Albania, the Albanian government was determined to find Pjeter Qafa and eliminate him. By now, Qafa was a folk hero among Albanians. The military had no idea where Qafa was hiding. The communists were doing everything they could to pinpoint his whereabouts. Offers of money and threats to citizens lives did nothing to influence anyone in assisting the government.

Pjeter Qafa got word from the freedom fighters that an Albanian army captain and ten soldiers were stationed at the Drini River crossing into Kosovo.

The captain's orders from Tirana were to find Qafa and capture or kill him—to end his continued work against the government once and for all.

Qafa had become a subject of folklore and songs which Tirana wanted ended. One of the songs, which made its way throughout Albania, heralded Pjeter Çup Qafa's exploits in his war against the communists. Another song celebrated the Qafa family. Here are theAlbanian versions. Unfortunately, they lose much of their meaning when translated to English.

They are printed here in Albanian for the pleasure of those who can speak the language.

Pjeter Çup Qafa song:

♪ N'bajrak Spaçit nzemer t'Mirdites
Po knojmë kangen e qiftelisë
N'shpinë e Qafes shpi me za
Brez mbas brezi pushka sju nda ♪

♪ Tash do fjalë te Qiftelisë
Po knojmë kangen e historisë
Pjeter Çup Qafa qe betue
Komunizmit mos me ju dorzue
Mal në mal ë pritë në pritë
Lufton trimi neper Mirditë ♪

♪ Pjeter Çupi ky far trimi
Mos me ra ndorë t'komunizmit
Poj thotë Lizës mori grue
Merre cucen hajde me mue
Komunizmi sot don alltin
Bash si bushtra i ka mbledh klysht. ♪

♪ Për Kosovë ashtë nise me shkue
Po don drinin me kalue
Vajza vogel nji vjeçare
Fort Po qan spoj dihet qare
Hidhe ndri gruse i ka thanë

Sigurimi se kapte gjallë ♩

♪ *Nji nga nji vitet kaluen*
Shpinë e Qafes e internuen
Diktatori djalli shqypnisë
Quan armiq djemt e Mirdites
Pse Nuk deshten komunizmin
Filloj koha persekutimit ♩

♪ *Ditë për ditë luajshin femija*
Shumë krenar rriten rinija
Tuj rujt Besën kusherinit ti
Del Pal Qafa nji burr zotni
Perkujron bukën Mirdites
Emni Palit dritë me diell... ♩

Nrec Nue Qafa song:

♪ Paska mbledh Serbi ushtrinë
Me pushtue donë Malsinë
Deklarue paska nji fjalë
Nuk ka kush para mu dal. ♬

♪ Kanë nisë rrugën tuj vazhdue
Dojnë Qaf Malin me kalue
Mirë por keq kishin llogaritë
Nrec Nue Qafa ju doli n'pritë ♬

♪ Bijt e shkines ma kadal
Se me ju i Kam dy fjalë
Se i kamë do djem me mue
Me pushkë ndorë flasin me juve ♬

♪ Prite shka pushken Mirdites
Se çka tgjen ti se ke ditë
Nrec Nue Qafa hollë po qet
Me kaj plum ka dy poj vret ♬
♪ Pjeter Qafes poj qon fjalë
Mos ta nalim luftën vëlla
Ma merr Zefin mos tleshojmë printen
Se për tgjallë skorisë Mirditen ♬

♪ Po flet Nreca kadal dale
Isa Begut i kam dhanë fjalen
Nu bofte gjaku me rredhë ne kroje
Nuk ka Serb qe shkel këto troje ♫

♪ Ashtë que nkambë krejt Qafa Malit
Fjalë e Besë Ismajl Qemalit
Avni trimit e Bajram Currit
Ka dhanë Nreca Besën e burrit
Pjeter Qafa thrret Frrok Lleshin
Qe kurr buza nuk ju qeshi
Me Çup Qafan bese kan lidhë... ♫

Qafa decided to wait for the captain and his men to leave so he could cross the river with two-armed guerilla fighters, his friends, Hida and Deda.

After three weeks, the captain and the soldiers were still guarding the Drini crossing. Faced with starvation, Qafa made his move. Deda suggested they go into the nearest town and have a gun battle, dying in a shoot-out with the soldiers of the army rather than starve to death. Hida agreed.

Pjeter Qafa instructed his men, "Follow my lead, and do not speak one word."

Dressed in his army general's uniform, Qafa went up boldly to the captain on the banks of the Drini River.

"Comrade Captain, you are to take me and my men across the river on your pontoon boat immediately,"

Pjeter Qafa ordered.

The captain replied, "Sir, I cannot cross with you unless you show me your paperwork to cross over."

"Stand at attention when you are addressing a superior officer, comrade captain. We are a special security unit. We have our orders, but we must cross the river immediately. Cross me and my men over this river right now, or I will show you who I am," Qafa bellowed.

"Respectfully, sir, I need to see your paperwork."

"Get going. I am pressed for time. I will show you my paperwork when we reach the other side," Qafa yelled.

Qafa was carrying an AK-47 under his arm, and his men had their machine guns at the ready.

Reluctantly, the hapless captain loaded his men, as well as Qafa and his two men, onto the pontoon. As they neared the other side of the Drini, Qafa quietly pointed out a rock wall to his men, instructing them to go behind the rocks and lay down and prepare to fire upon the soldiers.

Upon landing, Qafa's men dutifully took their places behind the wall of rocks.

"Now, sir, your paperwork please," the captain muttered.

Qafa took the AK-47 from his shoulder. He pulled the captain away from his men.

"Captain, my paperwork is all in order, and it is right here," Qafa said as he pointed the nozzle of the automatic rifle into the captain's gut. Qafa continued, "Now, do you want to die right here and now, or let me go? It's your choice. Do you see my men with their guns? They will slaughter you all, and I'm not afraid to die. I advise you to order your men to lay down or I will raise my hand. If your men do something stupid, they will be cut into shreds, as will you."

The captain, assessing the no win situation, ordered his men to stand down.

"Whoever you are, just go!" the captain blurted.

Qafa and his fellow rebels made a quick, bloodless exit into the safety of Kosovo.

Dede asked Pjeter why he didn't kill the captain and his men.

"He helped us, didn't he? He did us no harm, and there was no threat. He is in enough trouble without my killing him. The captain will likely be shot for dereliction of duty by his communist superiors anyway."

This showed Pjeter's reasoning and courage as a leader of men who was not bloodthirsty. He would only shoot to kill in self-defense.

Three years later, word had gotten back that the captain at the Drini crossing was executed by firing squad soon after their encounter—for not fighting and killing Pjeter Çup Qafa and his men. The story was told around every campfire throughout Albania and Kosovo, and the legend lived on.

Qafa felt badly that the captain was killed because of him, but he knew there was no choice in the matter. This was war.

Still another story that added to the legend of Pjeter Çup Qafa took place in the town of Fushë-Arrëz, the Qafa family hometown.

It was known that the Sigurimi had infiltrated the

area in their search for Pjeter. One afternoon, Pjeter's wife, Liza, had helped him to dress as a woman to allude the Sigurimi and escape from the town to the safety of the mountains.

Carrying a bundle of firewood on his shoulders, Pjeter kept his head low under his *rrube,* the long, dark scarf that covered his head. Hs wife's long dress, sandals, and shawl made him look like an average local woman.

As Pjeter was passing the small home of a friend of his wife's, unbeknownst to him, the Sigurimi were inside the house doing surveillance of the town. The woman of the house, seeing Pjeter walking with the wood and knowing that Pjeter was in mortal danger, opened the door of her home and stepped into the front yard.

"Liza, I am sorry, I'm too busy to have coffee with you today. I am very busy doing my chores," the woman shouted.

Knowing this was a signal of an impending threat, Pjeter Qafa, who was armed only with a handgun, slowly laid the wood bundle onto the ground near the home, kept his head well covered, and walked slowly to safety.

It is said that the bundle remained in that place for a long time for fear that the Sigurimi would find out Pjeter was the one to drop it and arrest his associates. Others say the wood was in its place for decades as a quiet monument to the legend of the great Pjeter Çup Qafa.

Author's Note: While doing research for this book, reading about the Qafa family, interviewing dozens of people who are aware of the legend of Pjeter Çup Qafa, and even some who knew him personally in Albania, Kosovo, Montenegro, and Detroit, I realized that this great man was very much like the great American abolitionist, Harriet Tubman, who made thirteen missions risking her life and saved over seventy enslaved people using the underground railroad during the darkest period of American history.

CHAPTER FIVE

Immediately after he was found guilty of attempted murder of the two communist sympathizer brothers in Brooklyn, Simon Qafa was remanded to the infamous, dangerous, and overcrowded Rikers Island city jail in Queens, New York for thirty days.

The Department of Corrections now owned Qafa for three years. With any luck—and he would need plenty of that—he would be free after twenty-four months.

The thirty-day bid in the New York City jail flew by with one blip that cost Simon a week in the "box," the dreaded Rikers Island solitary confinement.

Some days had passed after he'd arrived at Rikers Island, and Qafa wanted to call his family back in Detroit.

To be expected, there is always a boss inmate of any jail or prison cellblock. A typical meathead who uses violence and intimidation as a badge of honor. Using the public telephone in the overcrowded blue and white cell block, Simon was confronted by the thug while trying to make a collect call. Most prisoners at Rikers Island would make easy and inexpensive local calls, but in those days, an operator was needed to make a collect call to Detroit.

The inmate ran up to Simon with crazy eyes. "Did you

ask my permission to make your call?"

"I wanted to call my family. I didn't know I needed permission from a prisoner to use a public telephone," Simon calmly replied.

"I don't care who the fuck you want to call. Now you know my rules, get your fucking ass out of here before I fuck you up."

Simon decided he needed to stand up for himself or be a mark for this idiot and others like him.

"I went to the utility closet and broke off a piece of a wooden mop handle. I held it behind my back and returned to the phone, waiting for the jerk to approach. This time, the guy rushed at me with his mouth open and drooling. *Wham*, I bashed the piece of wood and split the guy's forehead, splattering blood all over the floor," Simon recalled.

The correction officers, known as CO's, grabbed the wounded inmate and took him to the jail's medical unit. Other CO's quickly carted Simon off to the box.

This action didn't play out entirely too well for the young Qafa. But then again, it ultimately worked out in Simon's favor.

Earlier, the word was that Qafa would be sent to a minimum-security prison where life was generally easier than tougher maximum-security houses. After the thirty days at Rikers, Simon was sent for a twenty-day evaluation and classification at the Fishkill, New York State Correctional Facility. At Fishkill, the prison system would determine where Qafa would spend his sentence. His splitting the Riker's bully's head open would be enough to send Qafa to the maximum-security Clinton prison at Dannemora, in upstate New York.

However, word that Simon Qafa was a man ready to defend himself had reached both guards and inmates at Clinton.

There is a pipeline of information in the prison world. Qafa's reputation first as a shooter and then as a man who didn't take any shit at Rikers certainly gained him some early respect, especially from his fellow inmates.

"The first thing they did to me at Clinton was shave my head and give me the dos and don'ts of life in this prison. There were a lot of rules and regulations, but to never put your hands on a CO was the number one rule. I was then assigned Section F, cell 13."

Prisoner 79A1377 was now an official prison inmate.

***

Depression hit Simon immediately. Here he was, incarcerated at a young age, surrounded by real criminals, his soccer career likely ended, while his family was in Michigan, still in danger from a blood vengeance. The future no longer looked so bright.

Qafa lamented his life every single day for the entire time he spent in prison.

"The depression really hit me hard. For one week, I couldn't hear. I literally heard nothing. Inmates talking, music playing, doors slamming. I heard no sounds at all. I was totally deaf. That lasted an entire week. My hearing slowly began to return as I adjusted to prison life. I was a total basket case. I think my brain had just shut down my hearing as a defense mechanism," Simon theorized.

It was no wonder that Qafa had bugged out.

***

Just four years prior to the shooting that sent him to his prison cell, Simon Qafa was in the seminary in Vatican City, studying to be a priest in the Roman Catholic Church.

At sixteen years old, living in San Biagio, Italy where Simon and his family had sought political asylum as Albanian refugees, Simon befriended a thin, bespectacled, Albanian-born Catholic priest by the name of Dom Prek Ndrevashaj.

Dom Ndrevashaj himself was a study in faith and bravery, impressing Simon Qafa and his father Pjeter. In his early life, Ndrevashaj first served as a teacher in Dajç, then in Burrel and Mat, places in Albania that, under communism, looked more like prisons and concentration camps than towns.

Ndrevashaj followed his calling to the priesthood and settled in Tirana, studying philosophy and theology. In Tirana, Ndrevashaj was imprisoned by the communist regime and taken to the Shkodra prison where he eventually managed to escape. Together with his mother and sister, Ndrevashaj crossed the Albanian border and entered Yugoslavia. In 1961, after serving as a teacher in Gusi, Montenegro, he enrolled in the papal Urbaniana University in Rome and fulfilled his desire to become a priest. In December of 1961, he celebrated his first Mass as a priest.

On orders from his superiors in the Vatican, Dom Ndrevashaj started the priestly mission as a chaplain for the Albanian political refugees who fled to San Biagio shortly after his ordination.

In San Biagio, Dom Ndrevashaj took the teenaged Simon Qafa under his protective wings. When Simon's family expatriated to the United States, Simon went to Vatican City that very day.

"It seemed like a total nightmare to go from studying to be a priest in the Vatican to being in a prison for attempted murder," Simon would later recall.

The depression that Simon felt in his prison cell at Dannemora reminded him of the despair he felt the first night he spent alone, away from his family at the seminary in Vatican City. Simon had never spent a night outside of the Qafa home until then.

"I never even saw a television until I was fifteen years old in San Biagio, and now, I was in Rome, thinking I would be a priest. What saved me while I was in prison, without a doubt, were prayers

and devotion to my faith," Simon remarked.

However, Simon Qafa never had a true religious calling to the priesthood.

"Honestly, at a very young age, I was attracted to the authority and the power the priests had among the people. I also liked the black clothes and the cassocks and the pageantry of the priesthood, but I never felt the real passion of becoming a priest. I really very much wanted to have my own family one day and live under freedom," Simon confessed.

While in the seminary, Simon met and befriended a man that would affect his life forever—a young Italian prelate, Father Angelo Comastri.

Simon studied philosophy for four years before he decided to leave the seminary.

Now he found himself in a six-by-twelve prison cell, depressed and regretful about what his life could have and should have been.

***

At the Clinton Correctional Facility at Dannemora, Qafa quickly gravitated to the Italian inmates, mostly gangsters and some mafia-made men from the Bronx, Brooklyn, and Queens, as well as criminals from his home city of Detroit.

"We would all eat together like a family. We made our own food. Mostly steaks, pasta with Italian sauce, and we made our own wine from leftover bread and orange juice. We buried the liquid underground for a few days, the yeast from the bread turning the juice into wine," Simon recalled.

"I played a lot of American football and soccer. I was a kicker for the prison Green Machine football team. We played the black team one day, and after I made a field goal, the entire opposing line seemed to converge on me, flattening me and knocking me completely out. I thought a tank had hit me. When I got up, my eyes were twirling around in my head. American football was not for me."

"I became good friends with a man named Mel Lynch, a fireman from New York City who was involved in the famous Bronfman kidnapping," Simon recalled.

In October of 1975, Samuel Bronfman, the son of Edgar Bronfman, the founder of the multibillion-dollar Distillers Corp-Seagram Ltd., had been kidnapped by Mel Patrick Lynch and Dominic Byrne. Edgar Bronfman paid a 2.3-million-dollar ransom for his son's release, but the younger Bronfman was still missing.

Less than two weeks later, when he was arrested for his part in the kidnapping, Byrne informed the police and FBI of Samuel Bronfman's whereabouts.

When law enforcement officers of the FBI and NYPD invaded Mel Lynch's apartment, they found a loosely bound and blindfolded Samuel Bronfman lying side-by-side with Lynch on the living room sofa.

Lynch had testified at trial that he and Bronfman had been in a homosexual affair for a year and that Bronfman masterminded his own kidnapping, threating to expose Lynch's homosexuality to his family and the FDNY if he didn't assist in the "kidnapping."

Byrne and Mel Lynch were eventually acquitted of kidnapping but convicted of grand larceny.

Both men served less than four years in prison.

Simon Qafa recollected his friendship with Mel Lynch.

"At Clinton, I was assigned a job as a nursing assistant at the prison hospital. I worked from nine in the morning until three p.m. every day. I enjoyed the work. It was easier than most jobs inside the walls. Mel

Lynch spent a lot of time in the medical unit, and we became good friends. Over time, I noticed that Mel was always very calm and relaxed. Eventually, I asked Lynch how he was so cool. Mel said, 'I'll tell you, Simon, because I know you won't rat me out. If you do rat, I'll spend the rest of my time in the hole.'

"Mel told Simon his sister would smuggle Valium pills into the prison to help her brother cope with his anxiety and depression from the incarceration. Mel said if I would help with the smuggling, he would share the drugs with me. His sister would drop the Valium pills into a garbage bin when she visited, and I would retrieve them. My share of the contraband Valium broke my depression. I took one every night, which helped me to relax and sleep."

More important than the Valium was the friendships that Simon formed with other notable inmates, who protected him like he was family. One friend was Joseph Bonanno Jr. whose father, "Joe Bananas," was a scion of the mafia family that still bears his name today. The other was Anthony Provenzano.

Anthony Provenzano, AKA "Tony Pro," took a liking to Simon. They became great friends. Tony Pro was a capo of the New Jersey faction of the Genovese crime family. He was best known for his association and, as time progressed, not-so-friendly relationship with Jimmy Hoffa, president of the International Brotherhood of Teamsters Union. The powerful Provenzano was the president of the International Local 560 in Union City, New Jersey. Years later, his name was synonymous with the disappearance of

Jimmy Hoffa, but there was no evidence to indict him on any charges.

"Tony Pro took a liking to me, and we ate together every day. He was short and very powerful, both in strength and in his demeanor. When Tony Pro left Clinton, he made it clear that I was to be totally protected until I was paroled.

That is exactly what happened," Simon stated.

***

Simon's family knew how much he was suffering from his weekly calls home and the sporadic visits they made to the remote Clinton, New York prison. It was a difficult trip to make from Detroit. The Qafa family pooled their money, and with the help of friends, an appeal of the ruling denying his first bail attempt was made. Money meant nothing against the safety and happiness of the Qafa son, especially for the reason he had been incarcerated.

On March 11, 1981, a brief was filed to the New York Supreme Court in the Matter of Simon Qafa v Edward Hammock. Hammock was the head of the New York State Parole Board.

An excerpt from the petition for parole showed how serious his attorney was in attempting to get Simon released from Clinton.

Petitioner was convicted of assault in the second degree and criminal possession of a weapon in the second degree but was acquitted of attempted murder.

He was sentenced to concurrent terms of 0 to 3 years and given a minimum period of imprisonment (MPI) of 34 months, on each sentence, by the Parole Board. The reasons given by the board for its decision, which in turn was affirmed by the Division of Parole, were: "Nature of your criminal offense where you planned to cause the death of two people, where they were shot and received serious physical injury, and need for further institutional programming." Special Term annulled respondents' MPI determination and this appeal ensued. Given petitioner's convictions of two serious crimes, an MPI of 34 months was well within the board's guidelines. Furthermore, it being quite clear in the record that the board was aware of what charges he was in fact convicted of, its reference to his having "planned to cause the death of two people" did not equate to a board finding that he was accountable for attempted murder.

Despite brilliantly quoting several case law precedents, the petition to reverse the Board of Parole's decision not to release Simon Qafa early from his sentence fell upon deaf ears at the New York State Supreme Court.

CHAPTER SIX

While Pjeter Qafa, his wife, and his children were living in the safety of Kosovo, Pjeter was continually crossing illegally over the border into Albania. It was estimated that Pjeter Çup Qafa made over one hundred difficult and life-threatening trips leading the many refugees to freedom while avoiding the pursuing Albanian army until 1960.

By his bravery and determination, Pjeter's dedicated purpose was to gather Albanian families from under the oppression of communism in Albania and bring them to the safety of Kosovo.

The "Legend of the Mountains," as Pjeter was called, left his family for extended periods of time, risking his own life on every expedition. He would tell the fleeing families, and believed it with all his heart and soul, "One day you will all be free." And that day, after a good deal of sweat, blood, and tears, freedom did eventually come.

During the time of his anti-communist activities, the Qafa family children were told that their father had business trips he needed to take. Not even his family knew of his actual activities and whereabouts for fear they would be arrested and tortured for any information on Pjeter. The children knew better than to ask about their father's business. Liza Qafa kept a close reign on her children and made sure they knew nothing about their father's heroism.

Some acquaintances of Pjeter Qafa were given five-year prison sentences without a trail if they were merely suspected of having aided the anti-communist rebels in any way.

To add to the anxiety and turmoil in their lives, the Qafa family was being moved every three years by the cunning and brutal Yugoslavian government. The family were sustained by a mere 3,000-dinar-per-month stipend which was well below subsistence level at the time to adequately feed and clothe them.

The corrupt Yugoslavian government was given 30,000 dinar per month, per family from Geneva, only passing on ten percent of the funds to the Albanian refugees. To the ruthless government, those funds from Geneva were a steady income flow. They took the large share of the charitable assistance funds for "administrative costs."

Kosovan families would aid the Qafa family, and other refugee families in their impoverished condition, with meat, cheese, yogurt, wood, raki, corn, and grain to keep them sustained and alive.

Simon Qafa recalls some of the harsh living conditions from those difficult days: "We had a very small house without electricity and running water. I clearly remember having electricity for the first time when I was ten years old. Our family had a tiny kitchen and one bedroom with three beds. One bed for my mother and father, one for the boys, and one for the girls. The bathroom was in the back of the house, and my mother would warm water on the wood burning stove to give us a weekly shower outside. The shower was fine in the summer, almost a relief

at times, but not very pleasant in wintertime, as you can imagine."

Finally, with the help of Dom Prek, the Qafa family was accepted to immigrate from Kosovo to Italy with the economic aid of the Vatican Pontifical Office, the POA.

The Qafa family had suffered and sacrificed long enough. Pjeter Qafa had decided that immigrating to the United States after going to Italy would be best for the future of his family. They would know the taste of freedom as they'd never known before.

Pjeter took his family on the arduous train ride from Prishtina to Belgrade, Serbia, then to Trieste, Italy, and then to Rome. Seeing the beautiful Italian countryside on the bus ride from Rome to San Biagio gave the family hope for a new beginning.

San Biagio Saracinisco, St. Blaise of the Saracins is a twelve-square-mile mountainous town in the Province of Frosinone in the Italian region of Lazio. San Biagio is located seventy-five miles east of Rome and about thirty-one miles east of the town of Frosinone.

Simon recollects his feelings as a teenager: "San Biagio was an answer to our prayers. It was a poor, rundown mountain town, but it was like heaven to us. There were about fifteen Albanian refugee families when we got to San Biagio, and the wonderful and warm Italian people accepted us as lovingly as family.

They welcomed us with open arms, giving us bread, cheese, meat, and coffee. When the monthly money came to us from the Vatican through Dom

Brecha, we would, of course, repay the Italian families' kindness. We were all packed together in a crowded area with the typically small Italian houses, with their tile roofs. To this day, I love the look of the orange- and slate-colored rooves on homes."

"I remember the town had one piazza with a fountain where we took the water to drink and cook with. There was one doctor and one small church where we attended Mass. As kids, after our chores, we played soccer all day, and there was a bar that had ice cream, and occasionally, we would have some. The Albanian families would visit each other often, practically daily, and reminisce with stories of Albania and hope for the future. Some evenings, my father, who spoke some Italian, would sing, and play the *Qiftelia*—the Albanian

guitar-like instrument. I can still hear his playing in my mind to this day. Life was pretty good. We all missed Albania very much though. After all, it was the land of our blood."

After one year at San Biagio, the Qafa family was approved to immigrate to the United States as political refugees. Pjeter took the family to Stamford, Connecticut. Simon went on to the seminary at Vatican City.

CHAPTER SEVEN

Smitten by the power that priests had with the faithful and their sharp and elaborate vestments, sixteen-year-old Simon Qafa left the tiny town of San Biagio with his mentor, Dom Prek Ndrevashaj, and headed to Rome.

A driver was hired to bring Dom Prek and Simon to Vatican City. Together in a small Fiat automobile for nearly two hours, Dom Prek spoke about life in the priesthood, the sacrifices that had to be made, and the glory of preaching the word of Jesus Christ and hopefully, one day returning to help the people in Albania. Simon listened attentively, but the beauty of the passing Italian countryside was somewhat distracting to the impressionable teenager. Nevertheless,

Dom Prek's words were absorbed as Simon began his new life as a potential Catholic priest.

Simon met Dom Prek's mother, and with Dom Prek, they stayed in her welcoming apartment in Rome for two days until the young man entered the Seminaria Romano.

The massive campus of The Pontifical Roman Major Seminary at Piazza de San Giovanni in Laterano would become Simon's new home.

In 1970, Dom Prek Ndrevashaj continued, on orders from the Vatican, to oversee all the Albanian immigrants in Italy.

Dom Prek's work continued, and he traveled from Rome to San Biagio often to check on the condition of the displaced Albanian families.

One sunny afternoon in Rome, Dom Prek was sitting on his Vespa waiting for a red light to change. Suddenly, from out of nowhere, an Alfa Julia sedan violently veered out of an oncoming lane, smashing into Dom Prek, and sending him flying fifteen feet into the air. The Vespa was destroyed. The priest fell to the ground, fracturing his right shoulder. The Alfa Julia sped away into the busy Rome traffic.

Soon it was disclosed to Dom Prek that the accident was intentional. Through friends in the underground, it was learned that the Communist Albanian government had called for a "hit" on Dom Prek. The government wanted the priest eliminated to thwart his, and the Vatican's, efforts in protecting the ethnic Albanian immigrants.

Simon continued the story, "One day, soon after his shoulder began to heal, I was going to San Biagio with Dom Prek from Rome. Dom Prek pulled his new Vespa over on a bridge near San Biagio. He instructed me to stay with the Vespa. He walked under a bridge, which was off the road, and a minute later, I heard gunshots. I ran toward Dom Prek and to the sound of the shots. I was shocked to hear gunfire. Knowing that he was now in personal danger, Dom Prek had purchased a 635 Baretta handgun. Panicked, I asked him what the shots were about. Dom Prek showed me the pistol and in a matter-of-fact way said, 'I had to see how this thing works. Now I am prepared for them.'"

In typical Albanian fashion, the good priest, a man of peace and a man of God, knew that he had to protect himself to continue his work for his precious people.

***

The soccer field at the seminary abutted the orange-roofed campus. This was where Simon would show his talent, speed, and love of the game of "Calcio." When he wasn't praying, studying, or walking with other seminarians in the gardens and piazza of the world-renowned school, Simon was running on the soccer field and doing his best to stifle his lifelong dream of being a professional player. After all, how many Roman Catholic priests could play for a team and save souls at the same time?

It was here that the young, impressionable Albanian met a man that would influence him for the rest of his life.

Father Angelo Comastri was the man who most impacted Simon Qafa's life.

Angelo Comastri was born
in Sorano, Italy in the province of Grosseto in Tuscany. After his secondary education, Comastri attended the seminary of Pitigliano and the Regional Seminary S. Maria della Quercia in Viterbo. He continued his studies at the Pontifical Lateran University, where he earned a Licentiate of Sacred

Theology, and at the Pontifical Roman Seminary. In March of 1967, Angelo Comastri was ordained to the priesthood.

Simon recalled, "I had been walking around Rome in a kind of trance. It looked to me like a fantasy land of history, art, architecture, and religion. After all, until that time, I had spent my entire life in poor mountainous villages in Albania, Kosovo, and San Biagio, Italy.

I never thought I would see such grandeur, splendor, and beauty in my life. Intertwined with my loneliness, being away from my family, I felt extraordinarily blessed by being in Vatican City."

Simon continued, "Dom Carlo, the Father Superior of the seminary, formally introduced me to Father Angelo Comastri at the seminary. The moment when I shook his hand, then and there, I knew he was destined for greatness. Father Comastri had only been a priest for one year when I met him, and I saw his concern about me in his gaunt face and large, olive-like eyes."

"Simon, this is Father Angelo Comastri. He is now your spiritual father. Learn from him, and maybe one day you will follow in his footsteps,"

Dom Carlo, the head of the seminary, declared.

"Father Comastri befriended me not only as a seminarian, but as a person. His humanity poured from his soul. He was concerned that at such a young age, I would be lonely, and he was absolutely correct—until one day, he saw me playing soccer at the field next to the seminary."

"Simon, I know I don't have to worry about you

finding friends any longer. Seeing you play soccer, I'm not sure your calling to the priesthood will continue," Comastri laughed.

Simon laughingly replied, "Well, Father, we will find out in a couple of years."

The young seminarian had learned some conversational Italian during the year he had spent in San Biagio but

studying to be a priest was no joke. Simon had to learn proper Italian. As part of his studies, Greek and Latin were essential for the priesthood. He also had to learn French as a foreign study. French was considered the international language in those days.

"My head was spinning. I felt like I was in the boxing ring with Muhammad Ali," Simon quipped.

"I went to Father Comastri to complain about the difficulty of absorbing these languages along with my other studies. Father Comastri simply smiled at me and said, 'Simon, trust in God.'"

Simon remembers, "I studied as hard as I could. I learned the languages quickly but had the most difficulty with Latin. The tenses and the verbs were most problematic to me. I passed all my

exams, but just got by in Latin, so I took summer courses to become proficient in the ancient language of the church. By the end of that summer, I went for the first time to see my family in the United States, along with Dom Prek. I really needed to see them, and I needed a break from the books. I was very excited to see the great United States of America from all the photographs I'd seen and all the stories I had heard."

At JFK International Airport, Simon and Dom Prek were met by Pjeter Qafa, his mother Liza, and Simon's oldest brother. They drove to the humble family home in Stamford Connecticut.

"When I saw the massive buildings on the New York skyline, I fell in love with the United States of America at that split second. The sheer size of the buildings impressed me like nothing else I had ever experienced or was remotely

capable of imagining. I knew at that very moment; the priesthood would be a problem for me. My doubts began. I desperately wanted to start my life in the United States and raise a family. As I said, unfortunately I never really had a true calling to the religious life."

After thirty days, absorbing what the Metropolitan New York area had to offer, Simon and Dom Prek returned to Vatican City. After his one month stay in the United States, thoughts of New York City, his family, the freedom, and opportunity that was available in America were front and center and constantly on Simon's mind.

"On weekends in Rome, I took long walks by myself, thinking of what I really wanted out of my life. I never let anyone know what I was thinking. I walked to and around the Piazza Novona, lined with restaurants and stores, filled with tourists. The amazing fountains created by the masters, and all the artists milling around, selling their work, was breathtaking. I would walk to the Piazza del Popolo, watching tourists enjoying the scenery and parents walking with their children. I would go to Trastevere and see all of the fabulous young people, the bars, and eating spots in Rome, constantly imagining the New York skyscrapers and what life could be like there," Simon reminisced.

After some time of difficult and challenging continued study, and mind-numbing doubt, Simon was playing soccer for Almas Roma, an amateur soccer team. On one beautiful cloudless weekend afternoon, the seminarian Qafa scored three goals, leading his team to victory.

The day after the victory, Simon was summoned to Father Comastri's office. He had no idea why his mentor wanted to see him.

The priest's office had a high ceiling and was quite large, with mahogany wood on all the walls. Thick, gold-painted, wood crown molding surrounded the room. Gleaming green Terrazzo marble floors sparkled and made voices and noises echo throughout the room. Like Father Comastri himself, the office furniture was modest. There was a rich Cherrywood bookcase on one wall, filled with volumes in Latin, Greek, and Italian. A centuries-old mahogany desk stood with two matching wood chairs across from the priest's high back, leather chair and a large, wood crucifix fixed on the wall behind Father Comastri. On either

side of the crucifix hung a photo of a smiling Pope Paul VI and a portrait of Mother Theresa of Calcutta.

"Well, Simon. I see you have planted some roots," Comastri blurted.

"What do you mean, Father?" Simon asked.

"I haven't seen three goals scored like that in a very

long time," the prelate announced.

"You were there?"

"I heard that you would be playing for team Almas, and I decided to come and see for myself."

"You should have told me, Father." Simon smiled.

"Simon, my son. There are all kinds of vocations in this life. There are doctors, lawyers, plumbers, musicians, storekeepers, soccer players, priests. You will need to choose which vocation is right for you," Comastri stated.

Simon was taken aback by the guidance. Simon realized the priest sensed the developing doubt he was having. Simon thought for a few seconds and replied.

"Thank you, Father. I will meditate on your advice." The two prayed together for guidance.

Simon was indeed constantly praying and meditating on his future without pressure from Father Comastri.

"I was so impressed by this man. By his humility, by his love of his fellow man, and by his service to God. I told some fellow seminarians, 'One day, Father Angelo Comastri will be our pope.' Little did I know that my prediction would be very close," Simon offered.

CHAPTER EIGHT

In the early 1970s, Pjeter Çup Qafa's nephew, his brother's son, Pal Qafa, worked tirelessly on the family land, trying to make a living, to simply put food on the table and clothes on his family's backs. Ruggedly handsome, Pal stood five-foot-ten with a strong athletic build, and his full head of pitch-black hair was always neatly combed back. His Qafa-inherited, bushy dark eyebrows added to his striking good looks.

At first, Pal Qafa, a very bright and college educated man, attempted to fulfill a life-long dream of becoming a schoolteacher. This was the manner in which Pal hoped to help his country—by educating the young minds of his community.

The communist Albanian government, in their constant quest to capture and kill Pal's famous guerilla uncle Pjeter Qafa and disrupt and desecrate the legend of the mountains, deemed Pal Qafa to be a *kulak*.

The term kulak is derived from a Russian word defined under the infamous blood-thirsty communist leader, Joseph Stalin, as "wealthy peasants who own land and employ others." To the communists, this was too much capitalism for them to allow.

In Albania, the communists considered a kulak to be a person who was *persona non-grata*. So much so, that the landowning class in Albania was virtually wiped out soon after the communists took power in the mid 1940s. This action was directly out of the Marxist playbook. The kulaks of Russia were run out or executed in similar fashion.

By the government's decision and with no appeal, Pal Qafa was not allowed to teach in Albania, if for no other reason than his relation to the infamous insurrectionist Pjeter Çup Qafa.

After Pal Qafa was rejected as a teacher by the government, he became understandably upset. He soon became angry and vengeful. He decided to continue his celebrated uncle Pjeter's anti-communist work.

What was deemed as insurrection in Tirana, without fear of recrimination, Pal Qafa came out openly against the Albanian government and its oppression of its citizens. There is one famous story about what Pal did in the town of Fushë-Arrëz, the ancestral home of the Qafa family.

Fushë-Arrëz is a town a municipality in Shkodër County, northern Albania, surrounded by rolling hills and peaked mountains for as far as the eye can see. Along the wide and winding main road that leads into the town square, there are gray concrete walls that have deep pockmarks from age and weather. Atop the walls sit square, unassuming one- to four-story homes, where generations of families have lived their lives peacefully and prosperously. At least that is how things were before communism came, according to folks from this small town.

Pal Qafa had discovered from some friends and family connections in Fushë-Arrëz that there was absolutely no food available, and the people of his hometown were literally starving, even though the government had ample stores of food.

Without hesitation, Pal Qafa broke into the local government depot and helped himself to as many bags of grain, corn, and flour as was possible. Pal distributed the goods to the famished families so they could feed themselves and their children.

Within a day, the communist party had discovered Pal Qafa to be the thief.

Pal was imprisoned for three hard and miserable years without a trial.

After his release from prison, Pal would be jailed regularly, with or without cause, for subversion and sentenced to two to three months in jail each time. It was total harassment aimed at his uncle Pjeter Qafa, who was not careless enough to get caught by the communist party or their confederates.

For one infraction, Pal Qafa had dragged a communist party member into the middle of a street and beat him senseless with a club. The reason for the battering has been lost in the family oral history. This assault got Pal Qafa a six-month jail sentence.

Pal's younger brother, Marc, was sentenced to six years as a political prisoner due to his "association" with his brother and the rebels. No formal charges were made, no trial, no defense—just jail.

Pjeter Çup Qafa was still considered to be the

greatest threat against the government. The *Sigurimi* were working to extract information about Pjeter and possible bases where the legend and his compatriots were supposedly operating and hiding.

Pal Qafa would in no way cooperate with the Sigurimi and the government. Pal adamantly refused, under threats of imprisonment or death, to give any information on the rebel organizations activities.

Unbeknownst to the Sigurimi, in 1974, even though Pjeter Qafa was living and working for the past year in Detroit on an assembly line for Chrysler Corporation, Pal Qafa was arrested and falsely charged with subversion and found guilty. Not by a jury, but by a lone communist judge.

Pal Qafa was sentenced to death.

In 1975, six months after his sentence—only the Sigurimi would know under what torture Pal Qafa endured during those months—he was executed by firing squad. He left his wife and three young daughters. Pal Qafa was only thirty-six years old.

Pal Qafa was buried in an unmarked grave in the Puka mountains so no rebels or family members would make a shrine for him and his bravery.

It wasn't until 1984, nine years later, that Pjeter Qafa was told of his nephew's execution. Pjeter was devastated and inconsolable, blaming himself for his nephew's demise.

Thirty-six years later, Pal Qafa's grave was found in the vast Puka mountains. The family was told of the location by an eyewitness. His remains were exhumed and returned to Fushë-Arrëz where he was laid to rest in the Qafa family cemetery.

Simon recounts, "Now you know why I hate communists to my core, with all my heart and soul. They oppressed my entire country and killed my family members, my cousin, and two uncles, with no sense of justice. I wish I could do to them what they did to so many brave men, including my dear cousin Pal Qafa who was truly a good and decent man."

***

About the same time that Pal Qafa was being persecuted by the Albanian government, his cousin Simon Qafa was battling his own special demons. He knew with relative certainty that the priesthood would not be his future. However, he was not yet ready to make the decision final and pull the plug on the ministry of souls.

Around that time, His Holiness Pope Paul VI took a walk through a secret tunnel that led from the Apostolic Palace to the Seminary to have dinner with the future priests. Paul VI sat with Simon Qafa and four other seminarians over a simple dinner of macaroni with tomato sauce and salad. The pontiff spoke with Simon about the conditions in Albania and the terror that the priests in his country were living under communist rule. Many priests had been executed. The pope was aware of what was going on in the church in Albania and told Simon that he would be needed to return one day to his country to help the faithful. Simon was so impressed by meeting and being in the presence of the pontiff that his confusion about staying in the priesthood was compounded. He had no idea what to do at this juncture, but the call to raise a family was overwhelming him.

On November 27th, 1970, his Holiness Pope Paul VI was visiting Manila. He was the first pontiff to ever visit the large population of Roman Catholics in the Philippines. At 9:30 on that sunny morning, a maniacal Bolivian surrealist painter, Benjamin Mendoza y Amor Flores, dressed as a catholic priest, attacked Pope Paul VI as the pontiff disembarked from his chartered DC-8 jet at the Manila International Airport. Mendoza stabbed the pope twice in the neck with a *kris*, an asymmetrical short dagger, hitting either side of the pontiff's jugular vein. On both sides of the *kris* was the inscription *"bullets, superstitions, flags, kingdoms, garbage, armies, and shit."*[

The private secretary of Pope Paul VI, Pasquale Macchi, likely saved the pope by blocking Mendoza's arm. Paul VI suffered slight injuries to his chest. His papal cross was cut from around his neck. It was miraculous that Paul VI was not killed. Mendoza was subdued by monsignors Macchi and Paul Marcinkus and was subsequently arrested. The shaken seventy-three-year-old pontiff continued his official visit before returning to Vatican City.

Simon recounts an interesting story that occurred soon after the assassination attempt on Paul VI.

"It was around three a.m., and all the seminarians were awakened by Father Angelo Comastri and told to dress quickly. I asked Comastri, 'What's going on? Is something wrong? Where are we going?' He coolly responded, 'St. Peter's Square' with no other information. The nearly forty seminarians gathered near the Apostolic Palace. Suddenly, the pope's white limousine and cars with his bodyguards and Vatican Police entered the piazza. We all began applauding. We knew Pope Paul VI was attacked, but we never knew he was almost mortally injured. That information wasn't released until after the pope's death in 1978. The limousine came to a halt, and the supreme pontiff exited the vehicle. He came over to the seminarians, shook our hands, and blessed us all. He looked a bit tired and shaken, but he was smiling through his near-death experience. Father Comastri was thrilled with the pope's response to our presence and support. I couldn't believe that I had again met the pope face-to-face. It was another wonderful moment in my life."

"After the 1972 school year, I went once again to Father Comastri's office. This time I was not summoned. I went on my own accord. I went in to see my mentor with a heavy heart."

"Simon! Don't worry. Be calm, my son. I know why you are here and what you will say," Comastri blurted.

"How do you know, Father?" I asked.

"It is my job to understand people. Please have a safe trip and remember to always trust in God."

Simon's time as a seminarian had come to an end. He had a "Titolo di Viaggo" visa and flew via Al Italia airlines, once again, to JKF airport in New York. This time, only Simon's brother met him at the airport.

When he arrived at his parents' home in

Connecticut, Pjeter Qafa asked his son, "How long are you staying, Simon?"

"Permanently," was Simon's only response. There was no need for further discussion.

CHAPTER NINE

While being interviewed for this book, Simon Qafa became very emotional at times. Simon showed, love, happiness, laughter, bitterness, and anger. He was often brought to tears. Of course, his disdain for communists brought out the bitter emotions of a man who lost close relatives to firing squads without legal representation, to a totalitarian regime which also searched tirelessly and relentlessly to murder his father—even after his father had expatriated to the United States.

Another source of deep emotion was the poignant memories he had of Father Angelo Comastri, and the priest's amazing rise within the Roman Catholic Church.

After Simon left the seminary, life took him in various directions. Some were very good, and some were down a road less traveled, but as life goes and takes ahold of time, Simon fell out of touch with Comastri.

Comastri began climbing the ladder to greatness as Simon had prophesized to his fellow seminarians.

In 1971, Comastri was promoted to rector of Seminario Romano until 1979 when he was named pastor of the parish of San Stefano Protomartire in Porto Santo Stefano. He was also a distinguished member of the diocesan college of consultors and served as episcopal delegate for the seminarians residing outside of the diocese. He was also a professor of religion at the Professional Institute for Maritime Activities in Porto Santo Stefano.

In July of 1990, Comastri was appointed Bishop of Massa Marittima-Piombino by Pope John Paul II. He received his episcopal consecration in September of that year. He resigned as bishop for health reasons in March of 1994. Comastri had a serious heart disease.

If not for the counsel and caring of an Albanian-born woman, Anjeze Gonxhe Bojaxhiu, whom Bishop Comastri enjoyed a close relationship with, Comastri's life would have been cut short. The woman would later be called Saint Teresa of Calcutta.

The bishop's heart was failing rapidly. So much so that even a brief walk was difficult. He needed a serious heart surgery his doctors warned could result in death. The odds were high.

Comastri sought the advice from his sister in Christ, Mother Teresa.

The bishop was seriously depressed with his failing health when he met with the diminutive Mother Teresa.

"What is wrong, my brother?" the loving nun and future saint queried.

"My heart is failing, and I will likely soon die. There is a surgery that I can have, but I've been told by the doctors that survival is not certain. I will most likely die from the surgery," Comastri explained.

The future saint glared at Comastri with an

uncomfortable stare. "And you say you believe in God?" Teresa replied. The tiny nun continued, "You get on the telephone with your doctors this instant and schedule the surgery. Only God will

decide if you will live or die. How dare you doubt him?"

Teresa then handed Comastri a ring. He removed his bishop's ring and put it in his pocket, putting Teresa's ring on his finger.

Bishop Comastri followed Teresa's advice.

***

Following his successful heart surgery, Comastri was named president of the National Italian Committee for the Jubilee of the Year 2000 and placed in charge of the National Center for Vocations of the Italian Episcopal Conference.

Bishop Comastri was then named Territorial Prelate, with the title of Archbishop.

In February 2005, Pope John Paul II needed Archbishop Comastri back at the Vatican. The pope appointed Archbishop Comastri as President of the Fabric of Saint Peter, a demanding and important position overseeing the restoration of the Vatican. Comastri was also appointed Vicar General of His Holiness for the State of Vatican City, and Coadjutor Archpriest of St. Peter's Basilica.

Angelo Comastri preached the Lenten spiritual exercises for Pope John Paul II and the Roman Curia in 2003 and the meditations for the Stations of the

Cross in the Colosseum in Rome on Good Friday 2006. Upon the retirement of Cardinal Francesco Marchisano in October 2006, Comastri succeeded him as Archpriest of St. Peter's Basilica, a prominent position in the Roman Catholic Church.

After the death of the beloved John Paul II, Pope Benedict XVI appointed Comastri to cardinal in the consistory in November 2007, assigning him the titular church of San Salvatore in Lauro with the rank of cardinal-deacon. In addition to his main duties, he also served as vice-president of the Pontifical Academy of the Immacolata, and he had been a member of the Congregation for the Causes of Saints since 2008.

Cardinal Comastri participated in the papal conclave that elected Pope Francis after Benedict's unprecedented resignation. After ten years as a cardinal-deacon, he was raised to the rank of cardinal-priest in May 2018.

Cardinal Comastri informed his staff that upon his death he is to wear the ring Mother Teresa had given him when he is entombed. The cardinal still resides in Vatican City as of this writing.

With tears in his eyes, Simon Qafa said, "He was like a second father to me." That is truly an amazing thing to say from the son of Pjeter Qafa, the legend of the mountains.

CHAPTER TEN

While I was researching background information on the Qafa family, I had the wonderful opportunity to have dinner at Dominick restaurant in the Bronx, New York. This just happens to be my regular favorite Italian spot in New York City.

Before and after dinner, we had drinks and coffee at La Parisienne Café with the welcoming and wonderful owner, Dervish Jahjaga.

At dinner was Simon Qafa, Tony Vuksanaj, and Abdullah Nezaj. I must tell you that I've had the pleasure of dining with this same crew several times before and never knew the long ties these men and their families had, both in Europe and the United States. They never shared this information with me in the past. The fact that I was writing a book about the Qafa family piqued everyone's interest.

What I discovered during dinner was fascinating.

Dominick is a family-style restaurant with no menu and no check. The food is like we are eating in my Italian grandmother's kitchen, and the Albanian waiters are all friends to us. Charlie De Paulo, the owner, is a dear friend to all of us and treats us like family.

We sat at a rectangular table, no tablecloths, no

matching flatware, no wine glasses, nothing fancy at all, but the food has been consistently great for over forty years.

Tony Vuksanaj is a big man with a gravelly voice and a lovable kindness in his face that one finds infrequently in a lifetime.

Tony offered, "My family was from Montenegro, but I've known Simon Qafa for fifty years. I knew his father well. When I was a little boy, Pjeter Çup Qafa would come to my house and visit with my father, and they would plan their anti-communist activities before they took to the mountains and caves to help families escape to Kosovo and freedom."

My father, Llesh Vuksanaj, made many trips back and forth over the boarders to bring Albanians to freedom. Many of the trips were with Pjeter Çup Qafa. I heard my dad did 194 trips as a guerilla. He would go into hiding to Croatia and Serbia for weeks at time.

"Just like Simon, we lost family to these communist bastards. My father's cousin was summarily executed in the town square, and the commies read a statement over his body. When they were through, they declared this would happen to anyone who went against the government. Things like this were burned into our memories.

"We were also sent to San Biagio, Italy. After San Biagio, we were granted our papers, and the whole family flew to JFK, thanks to the kind people in Geneva. We were all political refugees," Tony commented.

"What was Simon like as a child?" I asked.

"I didn't hang with him much until both of our

families escaped to San Biagio in Italy. I was an altar boy attached to Dom Prek and would see Simon when I served Mass. Dom Prek was a cousin to my mother, so I was close to him as well, but Simon was going to be a priest and that trumped everything. One day, Dom Prek had gone to my father and said that he needed one of his four sons for the priesthood. That son would have been me. My father and mother had nine children, and dad reluctantly but firmly refused Dom Prek. 'I cannot separate my boys,' was father's response. Otherwise, I would have gone to the seminary with Simon. But I must tell you, we would play marbles after church, and Simon was very competitive and could shoot the marbles like no one else. He would leave with his pockets full of the other boy's marbles," Tony added, to laughs from Simon and Abdullah.

"Where did you settle in the United States?" I asked.

"A few months in Brooklyn and then we came right here to the Bronx, right down the street at Adams place to a two-bedroom basement apartment with all those kids my parents had."

"And eventually you joined the Air Force?" I queried.

"I'm going to sound corny, but yes, at eighteen I joined the United States Airforce to pay back what this country did for me and my family. I served four years and nine months and was going to re-up for a five-thousand-dollar bonus, which was a lot of money back then, but my father wanted me back home to help with the younger kids and go to work to help the family. 'Don't be fooled by this bonus. I need you here,' is what he commanded.

"Of course, when Simon lived in Detroit and then served time in prison, we didn't see each other, but when he moved to the Bronx again, we became very close."

Abdullah Nezaj, to this day, has the tall, slim build of an athlete. His serious demeanor breaks into a soft but manly smile when the past is remembered. At least until an event happened in the Bronx that changed his life forever.

Abdullah agreed with much of what Simon Qafa and Tony V. both had stated. San Biagio was like being in another world. Freedom was precious to these people.

The people of this small Italian town had embraced the Albanian refugee families, making their stay as comfortable and happy as possible until they could immigrate to the United States.

Arif Nezaj, Abdullah's father, was an educated man with a degree from Belgrade University in Political Studies. Arif had been as determined as Pjeter Çup Qafa was to fight the communist regime in Albania, and the two men, one highly educated, and one not schooled at all, fought side by side in the Kursi mountains.

Abdullah and Simon now have a fifty-five-year friendship. As young boys, not even having a soccer ball, they recall using a basketball, sent from the United States in a CARE package. They played soccer in the rocky fields of Kosovo when taking breaks from working the land.

The glistening in both men's eyes as this remembrance was being told attests to the story's truth.

Abdullah recalls, "Simon and I both played mid-field, and when they formed the New York Eagles soccer team around 1978, we recruited the best player in Detroit at that time. Simon Qafa was that player. We knew each other so well on the field, we understood each-other's moves and motivated the entire team.

We had players from Argentina, Haiti, Yugoslavia, and Guatemala. One time we were on opposing teams and jokingly were pushing each other. The referee gave us each a yellow card. We were both hysterical with laughter. Our coaches were not."

Soccer was a means to an end for Abdullah Nezaj. He played the game for the Cornell University team where he was in a starting mid-field position. Studying Agricultural Economics at one of the finest universities in the United States could open many doors for the young Albanian.

"It was very hard for me. The soccer schedule was rough enough, and I didn't speak English, so I had to learn the language to compete in a difficult academic program. I hung in there and excelled with the help of God," Abdullah states.

"Then I was drafted by the New England Oceanas to play ball for them and for the Los Angeles Aztecs of the North America Soccer League. I decided that I was going to start working in New York instead and declined the professional drafts in favor of building my business. I was doing incredibly well in real estate and other endeavors until an event destroyed my plans . . . and my life."

On February 7th, 1987, The New York Times Metropolitan sections lead story read:

U.S. Agent is Shot During Drug Raid in Riverdale

That day coordinated raids were made in the Riverdale section of the Bronx by the Bureau of Alcohol, Tobacco, and Firearms after a yearlong investigation of a multimillion-dollar distribution ring in New York City and New Jersey.

Abdullah recounts the harrowing story:

"I was sleeping on my sofa when suddenly, the door to my apartment was being bashed in. There were drug dealers in the neighborhood and building where I was living, so I kept a .38 pistol close. It seemed that every Albanian had a gun. I guess a carryover from our roots. The door was suddenly shattered open, and I saw a male figure rushing in. I fired several shots. Evidently, I hit the guy who was breaking into my apartment because he came at me like a drunk, twisting around and falling right in front of me.

"I was trying to move upstairs to safety, a hail of bullets came at me. All I saw from the open door were hands and guns, with bullets whizzing by me. I could have very easily been killed. I ran upstairs and waited. I still had no idea it was the police until I heard two-way radio communication, sirens, and police screaming orders. The police were searching for me with vengeance.

"I jumped in a bed and lay there quietly, but my heart was beating through my chest. I knew I was surrounded. I also knew I would be gunned down by these cops, so I called 911 from the telephone in the room."

"Do you know about the problem on 246th and Henry Hudson Parkway?" Abdullah asked.

"Yes," the dispatcher responded.

"Well, I'm the guy they are looking for," he said.

The dispatcher replied, "Don't get nervous. How old are you?"

He stayed calm and said, "Listen, stop asking me silly questions, and connect me with someone in command."

After some back and forth on the phone with the local precinct, a captain finally made the arrangements for Abdullah's surrender.

"When I left the building in handcuffs, there were robots, helicopters, dogs, and an army of cops and detectives. All of the local media trucks were there broadcasting the event nationwide."

Abdullah had Anglicized his name to Adam for business purposes. Soon, the name Adam Nezaj was like John Dillinger or Machinegun Kelly in the New York City metropolitan area.

"I was in a police car in the middle of two beefy cops with two cops in the
front seat. Three squad cars were in front, and three cars were behind the car I was in. They drove very fast to central booking in lower Manhattan. One of the cops said, 'When we get there, we are going to beat the shit out of you.' I said, 'Make sure you do it!'"

Abdullah, AKA Adam Nezaj, was charged with

attempted murder of a federal agent in the second degree, and illegal gun possession. The federal agent was shot in the face.

"The big mouth cop never beat the shit out of me. I wanted him to beat me so I could show police brutality to the media. There again, I was using my brain to help myself."

Abdullah was booked at Metropolitan Correctional Center, and bail was set at $500,000. Within a few days, family and friends arranged to post the bail by putting some cash and properties on the line. That was an amazing amount of money back then.

Abdullah, if found guilty of these charges, could have faced over twenty years in federal prison. After some gut-wrenching time, a federal judge dismissed the case because there had been no warrant to enter Abdullah's apartment.

But the saga doesn't end here. The federal prosecutor tried several tricks to get the case reopened and was thwarted by the judges. The feds falsely claimed that Abdullah was a central figure in the Columbia Drug Cartel and was a sharpshooter for the cartel for the Northeastern United States. Total nonsense and fabrication, which the judges saw through and found in Abdullah's favor.

The State of New York took over the case on the gun charge and was seeking seven years in prison for Abdullah.

Abdullah added, "Tony Vuksanaj and my brother thought I should fight the gun charge, but I had already done a lot of time and took a two- to four-year plea bargain. I did a year at Rikers, which didn't turn out badly for me. Everyone knew I was the guy who shot a federal agent, and that was a badge of honor in jail, and the blacks welcomed and protected me. Aside from that, I am Muslim with a Muslim name. The blacks respected that."

Abdullah spent his time at the Oneida Correctional Facility in upstate New York. He was granted parole on the first try.

Two of the three Albanian refugee boys—Simon, Tony, and Abdullah, all friends from childhood whose fathers risked their lives to save their fellow countrymen—would wind up doing prison time for different and complicated circumstances. Tony Vuksanaj also had a brush with the law, but that's a story for another time.

CHAPTER ELEVEN

After he had served his time in prison, Simon Qafa was trying to reset his life. He wanted to put his past behind him and move forward. Simon wanted to live a good life as he had for most of his life.

***

It was July 30th, 1982, and Simon was at a soccer camp in Scottsdale, Arizona. Playing professional soccer was still on his mind and still a distinct possibility for him. He still had the agility and speed he needed to compete on the professional level. This camp was on the radar of several professional soccer teams that could scout players with Simon's skills.

With his gregarious personality, athletic build, and good looks, Simon didn't have difficulty meeting women. At that time, Simon was seeing a girl whom he cared for, and he was having a great time playing soccer and loving the nightlife.

Simon's niece had invited him to her wedding back in Detroit, but he wasn't sure he wanted to break camp on a Wednesday to attend her Sunday wedding. He was leaning toward not going. It wasn't until late in the afternoon of the 30th that Simon finally decided to get on the plane to attend the wedding and see his family and friends. It was a last-minute decision that would change his life forever.

His niece's wedding would be a small affair in the Polish Hall in

Hamtramck, Michigan, a town surrounded by Detroit.

"When I arrived, I looked around the reception hall like a wolf looking for his prey. I spotted this gorgeous girl with beautiful, light, very curly hair. I was immediately smitten. I literally couldn't take my eyes off her. I asked some friends who she was. One friend from Albania said her name was Lisa.

"In those days, I will admit, I was looking to add notches to my belt with as many girls as I could. I just wanted to have some fun. After all, the girlfriend in Scottsdale was just a play-friend and nothing serious.

"I made my way over to introduce myself to this beautiful creature of God. Lisa was sitting with her mother and father and other family members at a large round table."

"Hello, my name is Simon Qafa," Simon blurted.

Lisa responded, "I know about you. I heard you're a bad boy."

Lisa's father glared at Simon. He wasn't thrilled that Simon had approached his lovely twenty-year-old daughter. After all, the men he'd shot in Brooklyn were friends of his, even though he wasn't pro-communist. The entire Albanian community in the United States knew of Simon Qafa.

"Lisa and I chatted for a while, and I asked her if she would share a bottle of champagne with me. She accepted the invitation. The wedding hall had a cheap champagne—Andre, as I recall—so I excused myself and went to a nearby liquor store and bought a bottle of chilled Moet & Chandon. I wanted to make my first impression a good one. I quickly returned to her family table under the watchful eyes of her parents and family members, and we started drinking the champagne. We exchanged stories about her living in Washington Heights, in the north of Manhattan, and working at J. Walter Thompson advertising agency. At that time, it was the largest ad agency in the world. Lisa had a great job.

"Lisa's skin was like a porcelain doll, absolutely perfect without so much as a blemish. If her dress was fifteen dollars or fifteen thousand dollars, she looked utterly radiant. I asked if she would have lunch with me when I visited New York, and she accepted.

"Something had told me to come to this wedding in Detroit, and now I knew what that something was. It was fate pushing me. I knew then and there that the girl in Scottsdale was history, and I would be pursuing Lisa.

"After a while, and not to outwear my welcome, I took half the bottle of Moet and returned to my table. Lisa and I were looking at each other from across the room, so I got up and politely asked her to dance to one of the Albanian songs, to a traditional Albanian dance. I discovered from Lisa that she was staying with family in Detroit for three days, so I asked her to join me for dinner the next night. She accepted but, of course, only under strict Albanian customs. No courting was allowed if we were alone. That could never happen. Her cousin Angie would be our chaperone for the evening, and that was fine by me.

"We went to a great Italian restaurant called Francesca's where we met at 6:30 that evening and ended the dinner at 9:30.

"Without a doubt, we had the most intelligent conversation I'd had in my life. She was not only strikingly beautiful, but she was also very sophisticated and smart. I thought she was just perfect for me. We made plans to see each other again for lunch in New York."

The next week, Simon said goodbye to his girlfriend, left the soccer camp, and moved back to Detroit from Arizona. He made several trips to New York, staying at the Roger Smith Hotel on Lexington Avenue and 47th Street to be close to where Lisa worked.

"On one of those visits, I was thinking about adding Lisa to my belt notches, so I asked her to come to my hotel room.

Lisa replied, 'I'm never going to your hotel room. You can forget about that idea. How dare you even ask?" Lisa was a bit angry with me. She put me in my place immediately and, of course, I backed off, apologizing for my faux pas. After one full year of this courting, I finally told Lisa that I was falling in love with her. I told her I was in love for the first time in my life. Her reply was amazing. 'What took you so long?'"

Simon continued the love story. "I knew Lisa's father didn't care for me because of my past, so Lisa said she would talk with him. I then returned to Detroit and asked my father to visit New York so he could ask her father for Lisa to marry me, as is the Albanian custom.

"Three families had already asked for Lisa to marry their sons, but Lisa told her father, 'I will not marry anyone but Simon Qafa.' Her father wasn't at all happy with her decision, even though her father and my father were old friends.

"I went back to Detroit and drove my father to New York to visit Lisa's dad and ask for her to marry me.

"Over coffee, another Albanian tradition, Pjeter Qafa said, 'Pjeter Bucaj, you know why I am here. I am here to ask for your daughter, Lisa, to marry my son, Simon. I must tell you as a friend that if you knew my son as I do, you should hesitate, and there will be no insult taken on my behalf.' I was shocked by my dad's words.

"'Pjeter Bucaj replied, 'How can I say no to you, Pjeter Qafa? Because of you, I will say yes. My daughter will follow your son to hell if need be.'"

***

Four months later, On September 29, 1984, Simon Qafa and Lisa Bucaj were married in Our Lady of Shkodra Albanian church in the Bronx, New York.

Immediately after the ceremony, the newlyweds went to La Guardia Airport and flew to Detroit for an Albanian wedding with over four hundred family and friends in attendance.

CHAPTER TWELVE

Before he was married to Liza, Simon Qafa was released from prison for shooting the two brothers in Brooklyn. He was paroled from New York to the State of Michigan because that was his last known address. He lived with his family until he could sort things out.

Finding a good, legitimate job for a violent felon is nearly impossible. Simon did odd jobs for a family of Italian descent with the blessing of Tony Provenzano, his Clinton prison friend and mentor.

Trust was one of the most important job qualifications for a job such as this, and Simon had the trust of the men at the top of the crime world.

His main job was collecting money for the well-known underworld family —which will not be named here— in West Bloomfield, Michigan. The family trusted Simon, and he would receive an ample weekly envelope in cash for his work.

One early morning, at four a.m. Simon was dispatched to an after-hours club to pick up an envelope. The club was at Detroit's Six-Mile and Woodward Avenue.

Simon parked the car outside the unmarked club and was approached by a homeless man who wanted twenty-five cents. The man's clothing was tattered and stained, and he reeked of booze and urine. Normally, Simon would chase the bum away, but he was tired and didn't want to be bothered. He handed over a quarter to the seedy, smelly man and began to walk toward the club door.

For some reason, the homeless guy evidently thought Simon was afraid of him. He became aggressive.

The disheveled man bellowed, "Hey man, now give me a dollar!"

From under his jacket, tucked in his waistband, Simon had a .38 revolver, a clear violation of his parole. He pulled the gun and put it into the man's face.

"I don't know what got into me. I just reacted quickly and without thinking. I said to the homeless man, 'Now give me my quarter back, you fucking asshole.'"

Simon checked the man's pockets and found seventy-five cents and took it. The man then ran across Woodward Avenue screaming, "That guy over there is crazy; he robbed me, and he has a gun!"

Simon went into the after-hours club where he saw Vito, the manager.

"Do me a favor, Vito. Hide this gun; I just robbed a homeless guy," Simon announced.

"You have an envelope here with a grand in it. Why the fuck would you rob a homeless guy?" Vito asked.

"Long story," Simon offered. He took the envelope and went to his car.

"I could have been apprehended with the gun and sent back to finish my prison sentence for this stupidity," Simon later recalled.

"I drove my car North toward Eight-Mile, all the while sweating and trembling, looking in my rearview mirror for a cop car or an unmarked police car. I was lucky I wasn't followed. I got home and couldn't sleep, constantly going over the scene and asking myself how I could have robbed that poor guy? I still can't imagine why I would have done such a stupid, boneheaded, spontaneous thing."

It seemed Simon's personality was going through a transformation of some kind. Not that long ago, he was in Rome at the seminary studying to be a priest.

Was rolling that homeless man with a gun for seventy-five cents the smartest thing a man on parole should do? It seemed that Simon was angry at his situation in life and was crying out for something or someone to change his situation. This kind of life was never for him.

Soon after, another event underlined Simon's desperate need to put his life back on the right track.

It was Easter Sunday morning, and after Mass Simon had stopped at the Coral Gable Club on Woodward Avenue and Thirteen Mile in Detroit for a drink.

His .38 revolver was tucked safely and unseen under the driver seat of his car. Simon put a set of gold-plated brass-knuckles in his right front pant pocket. They were given to Simon the week before by a close friend who thought Simon could use them in his collection job, if for nothing else than a prop. Once inside, Simon ordered a Bloody Mary at the bar. He noticed a large group of motorcycle club guys at the end of the long, rectangular bar.

"I spotted a big tough-guy biker who was kicking the shit out of two Albanian guys. I wanted to come to the aid of the Albanians and just break up the situation. I approached the hard-breathing biker and tapped him on the shoulder from behind. This guy was huge. Way taller than me."

"I said, 'Look, why don't you just stop and leave those guys alone?' The biker put his finger in my chest and hollered, 'This is none of your fucking business. Get lost, or I'll do the same to you, asshole.' Again, something inside me snapped. I put my hand into the brass knuckles in my pocket, got on my toes, and hit this guy on the side of his jaw with all my might. A big problem then occurred, as he didn't even flinch. My punch was like a mosquito to him. He moved closer to me, and through clenched teeth said, 'Either you are stupid or very tough.' I replied with a smug answer, 'Maybe a little of both.'"

Simon threw a twenty-dollar bill on the bar for his drink, then made his move to get to his car. He was followed outside by the biker and his equally huge and equally stinky friend. Both were wearing identical denim biker vests over black t-shirts with white skull and crossbones decals. All four arms on the bikers were tattooed from knuckles to neck, and each guy wore a head rag bandana—red on the guy Simon had punched, and black on his partner.

Simon tells the story all these years later with detailed clarity.

"I moved quickly to my car with these two monsters

on my heals. If they grabbed me, I didn't have a chance. My hands were trembling so badly I couldn't get the key into the car lock. In those days, we didn't have electronic car openers. Just keys. Finally, with two hands to steady the key, I got the lock opened and jumped into my car. These biker guys were all over me and started to pull me out. They would have pounded me into the ground or maybe worse. I dropped to the floor of the car and pulled the .38 from under the seat. My hands were still trembling, but that was no longer a bad thing. I put the gun in the face of the guy I'd hit. He was stunned. Both huge bikers put their arms up in surrender. 'Can we leave, man?' the second biker asked. 'Yes,' I replied. 'Can I leave?' I asked. 'Yes,' was the exact answer I wanted to hear. 'Have a nice day, boys,' I blurted, and off I drove."

All Simon wanted that Easter Sunday morning was to relax with a Bloody Mary or two—or five. He could have shot someone and maybe even killed a man. At the very least, he could have been violated for having a concealed pistol and sent back to prison to finish two years of his original sentence.

Thinking clearly and no longer out of fear, Simon realized he could be reported by someone at the bar or the bikers themselves, or perhaps followed by random police. Simon threw the gun into some bushes on his route home.

The next day, after another restless night, Simon returned to retrieve his
gun. The .38 was exactly where he left it.

Simon didn't meet Lisa a moment too soon. He was headed down a road which would have surely destroyed him. A life he was not made for.

CHAPTER THIRTEEN

Soon after his marriage to Lisa, Simon knew he had to leave Detroit and begin anew in New York City, largely because Lisa's job was in New York, and she would be happiest around her family.

The added fact that Simon knew he was working a dead-end career with an organized crime family was enough to make up his mind to leave Michigan. After all, the mob has a terrible retirement program.

Simon and Lisa moved to a nice, large apartment on Cambreleng Avenue in the Belmont section of the Bronx. The neighborhood, at that time, was very safe, unlike much of the Bronx. Belmont was largely made up of hardworking second- and third-generation Italian and new Albanian immigrants. Belmont was also known to be a long-time core of the Bronx mob.

Because of his affiliation with the tough guys in prison in Dannemora and the with the mob in Detroit, Simon was befriended by the men who were in control of the rackets on Arthur Avenue, the hub of the Belmont section. It seemed as if Simon was gravitating to this world. Since Simon was "on record" with the Michigan mob, it seemed like a natural transition to work in that arena. Simon spent a lot of time with the wise guys around Arthur Avenue. For obvious reasons, no names will be mentioned here.

Because of the unresolved, ongoing blood feud that Simon had hanging over his head from shooting the two communist sympathizer brothers in Brooklyn, he carried an unregistered .38 pistol for his personal protection. He never knew when the vengeance of the men's family would come for him. It was never a question of if they would try to kill him, but more a question of when he would be attacked. Carrying a gun was the only viable means to protect himself from the ancient code of blood revenge that would go on for as long as it took the avenging family to complete. The males in Simon's family in Detroit were also armed and on constant alert for their safety. It became a way of life to carry a gun.

After a year being happily married to Lisa and spending time in the social clubs and restaurants in the neighborhood, one afternoon Simon was arriving home in his car after an appointment in Manhattan. Simon was pulled over by two detectives in an unmarked car for making an illegal turn. He could not have made an illegal turn on or near Cambreleng Avenue as there was no place to make an illegal turn. Once again in his life, Simon had been set up for trouble.

The detectives illegally searched Simon and his car, and, of course, they found his gun. The Sullivan Law in New York City made the penalty for carrying an illegal gun two years in jail at that time. Simon knew this could happen, but felt it was better to protect his life from the blood feud.

"They arrested me on the spot and took me to the

48th Precinct for booking. I was put in a small interrogation room that had a table and some chairs. One for me and two for the detectives. One of the cops said, 'You're screwed, Qafa. You are facing two years behind bars on this gun charge. But there is a way out.' I asked what that way out was. The second detective laid four black and white surveillance photos in front of me. The photos had me together with some of the well-known mob guys from the neighborhood. The second cop said. 'We know that you are around the men in these photos quite often. If you tell us about their various activities, we can very easily make the gun charge go away. They will never know of your cooperation with us. I suggest you save the time in jail and the embarrassment to your wife and family.'"

"I'm not your guy," Simon immediately replied.

"Then you will do the time," the first cop said.

"It's my time, not yours, so don't worry about it," Simon answered.

After posting bail, which was lent to Simon by friends and family, it took two years in the courts for Simon to be sentenced to the inevitable two years in jail on the gun charge. It was yet another blow.

"I spoke with Lisa and told her I would not stand in her way of she wanted a divorce or annulment instead of waiting for me. She laughed at the idea, telling me she would wait for me forever if need be. Two years was nothing."

So, she would not be grist for the rumor mill—a beautiful, young woman living alone while her husband was in jail—Lisa decided it was best to leave the

Cambreleng Avenue apartment and return to her father's apartment in Washington Heights. Simon was incarcerated in the Altona Correctional Facility in upstate New York.

The men Simon had protected were forever grateful for the young Albanian's silence and loyalty. Lisa was told by the wise guys that while Simon was away, if she needed money or if anyone was bothering her, she was to go to them for help—they would be insulted if she didn't. Lisa didn't need anyone's help as she was working and making a very good living in the advertising industry in Manhattan.

Simon returned to his faithful and loyal wife after only ten months of his sentence.

While he was in a half-way house and working for a friend in a printing business, Simon would visit his wife. Lisa became pregnant with their first child during that time.

In 1990, Jackie was born. Through friends, Simon got a job as a security man with the stately and famous Ritz Carlton Hotel in Manhattan. After six months on the job, Simon was made security supervisor. The future was starting to look much better for the Qafa family.

CHAPTER FOURTEEN

After a while, through friends, Simon obtained a good job in security at The Helmsley Palace Hotel.

Leona Helmsley, the wife of the real estate mogul billionaire Harry Helmsley, ran the Helmsley hotels with an iron hand.

The news media was never kind to Mrs. Helmsley, calling her, among other harsh names, The Queen of Mean. Her quote, "Only the little people pay taxes" did not endear her to most people, rich or poor.

Simon recalls, "So many people called her nasty and mean, but she was very nice and very professional to me. I can tell you an interesting story. The keys to her office were closely guarded and were always left in the security office. We had direct and explicit orders from Mrs. Helmsley that no one, under any circumstances, should ever take her office keys. One day, she was not expected to be in the office. I was wearing a beautifully tailored gray suit, a crisp white shirt with a solid burgundy tie, and two-tone brown shoes. If I say so myself, I was looking quite sharp. Mrs. Helmsley appeared at the hotel around two in the afternoon. She needed the keys to her office. I hurried and retrieved the keys from the security office and went quickly to Mrs. Helmsley to open her door. 'Can I do anything else for you, Mrs. Helmsley?' I asked."

"She replied, 'As a matter of fact, you can, Simon. Get your ass out to my town car, go home, change your shoes, and get back here as soon as possible. By the way, I like your shoes.' I did just as she said. I didn't know until that moment that two-tone shoes were a no-no in the hotel business."

Simon continued his Helmsley Palace Hotel stories. "Another time, Peter Gotti, the Dapper Don John Gotti's brother, asked me to get him an office in the hotel for a private meeting. He and some other Gambino wise guys spent a lot of money at the bar in the Palace. They were great customers, and eventually the family would have John Gotti Junior's wedding at a Helmsley Hotel. Peter Gotti would ask me from time to time to accommodate him with an office. Mrs. Helmsley wasn't very happy. 'Simon, this doesn't bring a smile to my face, but you have to do what you have to do in this business.'"

Simon left the Helmsley Palace for a better position and a higher salary back with the Ritz Carlton, one of the swankiest hotels in New York City.

"I would often see Mrs. Helmsley walking her small, white dog along Central Park South. She was living at the Park Lane Hotel at that time. One day she saw me and stopped to chat. 'Simon, I hope you and your family are all well. I can tell you one thing for sure. I never should have let you leave the Helmsley Palace. That was a big mistake on my part. You always have a home at the Helmsley Palace.'"

So much for the Queen of Mean.

Simon Qafa headed the security office at the Ritz Carlton, and for substantially more than he'd been making at the Helmsley Palace. It was a dream job for him with everything that had happened to him over the past few years. Like at the Helmsley Palace, Simon continued rubbing elbows with the rich and famous. He was quite comfortable with that element.

A famous sportscaster—who will not be named here, as he is still active in the sports world—was a regular guest at the Ritz Carlton. One morning, the sports commentator called the security office to file a report about a missing $10,000 Rolex watch.

Simon tells the rest of the story: "I went to his room and listened to him rant about the stolen watch. I asked him a pointed question. 'Was there anyone here with you last night?' 'Absolutely not, I was alone,' was the answer I received. I immediately went to the security office and reviewed the internal videos of the floor he was staying on. Sure enough, not one, but two women entered the sportscaster's room with him. I recognized one of the women as a crack addict prostitute from Sixth Avenue that we had encountered before. When I returned to his room, I asked him again. 'Are you sure you were alone last night sir?"

"Yes, I was alone, I already told you that," he said in an aggravated tone.

"Well, sir, I just reviewed our video cassette, and I saw you enter your room with two women. Are you certain you want to file an official report?"

"I got the message. Just forget about it," he responded.

The sportscaster never returned to the Ritz Carlton after that incident.

Another day, "I was on duty, milling around the lobby when I noticed a huge, very filthy homeless man pushing his way past the doorman. The bum accosted and pinned a guest, a young

man, against the wall. I moved fast, knocking the homeless man to the ground in one movement and handcuffed him behind his back. The police were immediately summoned, and the hapless bum was taken away.

"My general manager came to the scene. He asked me if I knew who the young man was. I had no idea. I only knew he was a guest by his luggage in the foyer. 'He is the son of a very big customer. The father is an international arms dealer by the name of McVey,' my boss said.

"I knew who Mr. McVey was. Whenever he was staying at the Ritz Carlton, none of the staff took a day off or called in sick. He would squeeze hundred-dollar bills into the hands of everyone on the staff whom he encountered. The doorman, the bellhop, the desk clerk, everyone got a hundred-dollar bill. About a week after the incident with his son, Mr. McVey came to stay at the hotel. The second he arrived; he asked the doorman who Simon Qafa was. I was called to the lobby on my two-way radio.

"When I arrived at the lobby, there was a short, stocky, bald man who looked Irish to me."

"Simon Qafa?" he asked.

"Yes, sir."

"I'm McVey. I wanted to personally thank you for helping my son on his visit here last week. You acted bravely, and I appreciate what you did."

"Thank you, sir. I was just doing my job," Simon uttered.

He handed over an envelope which Simon stashed inside his jacket pocket.

"When I got home that evening, I gave the envelope, with five thousand dollars inside, to Lisa. For three years, every time Mr. McVey stayed at the Ritz Carlton, he gave me an envelope with one thousand dollars in it. He offered me a job as his head of security in California for significant pay. I discussed this with my wife, Lisa. We decided that our family, friends, and Lisa's job were all in New York. I didn't take the job and regret it until this day."

Simon started some great friendships with certain celebrities. Among them was the fabulous A-list actor, Bruce Willis.

One night, Bruce caught Simon on his way out of the Ritz Carlton before, heading home.

"Simon, come on, let's go get a few drinks," Willis offered.

They went to a spot where Willis had been a bartender at one time. The actor told Simon of how he almost stayed as a bartender for life.

"Bruce told me that he was going to audition after audition in the acting world with no success. Finally, he decided that he would go to one more audition and if he didn't get the part, he would hang up the idea of being an actor and go back to this place and mix drinks for a living."

Fate had changed in Bruce Willis' favor. The audition was successful, and he got the part of David Addison in Moonlighting alongside the Maddie Hayes character played by Cybil Shepherd. The rest of Willis' life is a success story second to none.

"I also became quite friendly with Jerry Garcia and other members of the

Grateful Dead Band. They often stayed at the Ritz Carlton. For many years, Jerry would send a birthday gift of one hundred dollars for my daughter Jackie's birthday. When the band stayed at the hotel, Jerry would let me know when they were smoking pot—which was all the time—so I could disengage the smoke and fire system in their room. I was happy to accommodate Jerry. He was a very nice man with a heart of gold."

Simon had friendships with Madonna, the band Arrowsmith, Arnold Schwarzenegger, OJ Simpson, and a slew of other famous and infamous.

OJ would come to the Ritz Carlton with Nicole and their children whenever they were in New York. Lawrence Taylor, another football hall of famer, would pick OJ up in his SUV at the service entrance when they would go out together.

"One time, OJ was walking to LT's car near the service entrance when a street person yelled out, 'Hey, you, I know you man … you Jim Brown.' The look on OJ's face was priceless. I waited until I returned inside to laugh my ass off," Simon added.

Kim Basinger, the absolutely gorgeous blonde

actress, was dating Alec Baldwin at the time and was staying at the Ritz Carlton. She became friendly with Simon and relied on him to help her with some personal details when she stayed in New York. One day, she wanted a VCR installed to her television in the lavish presidential suite on the twenty-fifth floor. Kim asked that Simon bring the VCR unit to the suite.

"When I arrived, I could hear her yelling at someone in an argument. When she opened the door, my knees almost buckled. Kim was wearing a long, black, silk gown with a black silk belt around her waist. Her flowing, blonde hair was a vision from heaven. Kim was arguing with Alec Baldwin on the telephone, and the fight was getting very heated. Finally, Kim said, 'I have to go, a good-looking security man is here to fix my television.' And she hung up on Baldwin, who I could still hear screaming on the other end of the phone. I installed the VCR and started showing her how to operate it. She stood behind me, leaning down as I showed her the VCR. Suddenly, one of her precious boobs fell out of the black gown. I nearly shit myself. She plopped it back into her gown and said, 'Sorry about that, Simon.' I wanted to say it was my pleasure, but I kept my mouth shut for once."

The Reverend Louis Farrakhan of the Nation of Islam was a guest at the Ritz Carlton on occasion. On one particular visit, Simon Qafa escorted Farrakhan to a suite on the twenty-fifth floor. Simon was impressed by the nattily dressed reverend. Nice clothes and good grooming always made Simon take special notice of people.

With Reverend Farrakhan were two tall, well-built bodyguards in black suits and white shirts and ties.

When the elevator started to rise, one of the bodyguards stuck his finger into Simon's back, possibly checking to see if he had a weapon.

Simon recalls the story, "I said, 'If you do that to me again, I swear I will break your finger. What kind of bodyguard are you? You should have checked my waistband, because if I intended to do harm to the reverend, I would have had my gun in front of my waistband.' I turned to Farrakhan and told him he was wasting his money on such poor security. He smiled at me and said, 'Young man, I admire your guts. I apologize for the inappropriate behavior.' The next morning, the two bodyguards asked if they could talk with me. They came to apologize. I shook their hands and said the reverend had already set things straight with me. All was good."

One of Simon's favorite stories of the rich and famous was an altercation he had with the famed movie director Spike Lee. Simon had instituted a rule that anyone who was returning to the hotel after one a.m. would have to show their room key to gain access to the elevators.

"I was working the midnight shift as security and fire director. I was near the elevator bank when I saw this guy heading for the cabs. He looked like any disheveled guy that I routinely threw out of the hotel. Besides, I never knew who Spike Lee was, and I didn't give a crap either. Rules are rules. 'Excuse me, I need to see your room key before you can enter an elevator,' I said. This little guy then put his finger to my chest. 'Do you know who I am?' he blurted. I replied politely, 'If you are a guest of the hotel, then you should have a key. It doesn't matter who you are. Just show me the key.'

"Lee finally showed me his key, and I said, 'Have a nice evening.' He replied, 'You will be hearing from me.' The next morning, I was called into Mr. Mady the general manager's office. When I approached the office door, I could hear Mr. Mady and Spike Lee laughing it up. When I entered, they suddenly went quiet. I didn't wait to be asked to sit. I just sat in a chair next to Spike Lee and across from Mr. Mady.

"'Simon, I think you were way out of line to insist that Mr. Lee show you his room key,' Mr. Mady offered.

"I immediately went on the offensive. 'How dare you call me in here and say that to me? You pay me to keep our guests safe, including Mr. Lee here. I'd rather get fired than risk people's safety and not follow the rules. If you called me in here privately, maybe I wouldn't be so upset. So, tell me, should I go home, or should I get ready to start work?' Spike Lee smiled at Mr. Mady. Mady said, 'Okay, Simon, go do your job.' I got up, and before I left the room, I said, 'Oh, Mr. Lee . . . you still have to show your room key after one in the morning.' We all laughed out-loud."

In those days, Simon was like the prince of the city. He knew everyone who was anyone, and he was respected wherever he went. One day, he was in the lobby of the Ritz Carlton when a well-known mobster, entered the lobby with a beautiful girl half his age. Simon had his security earpiece and his two-way radio.

"Simon? How in the fuck did you get a security job? You of all people?" the wise-guy bellowed.

"Don't worry about it. I guess I got the job from someone at the Ravenite," Simon replied, alluding to the Gambino social club on Mulberry Street in lower Manhattan. They both got a big laugh at that quip.

One day, senior management of the Ritz Carlton decided that all senior security people needed to be fingerprinted. Unfortunately, Simon knew this was the end of his security career. He loved the job, but like many people do, he'd lied on his job application. And not a little lie, at that. Simon was a two-time felon with serious prison time under his belt.

Rather than be embarrassed and fired, Simon tendered his resignation due to "personal reasons." Hotel management offered him a significant raise in salary to stay, but Simon knew it was no use.

Once again, Simon's past had returned to haunt him and his family. Fortunately, he landed a great job as a property manager at Summerset House in White Plains, New York. An added benefit to the Summerset job was a rent- and utilities-free apartment. For the seven years he was there, he and Lisa saved enough to finally buy the house they always wanted.

Then, an event occurred that turned Simon's world upside down.

CHAPTER FIFTEEN

Life was treating Simon Qafa better than it had in many years.

Simon once again had a great job. This time at Sommerset House in White Plains managing the apartment complex. He had two beautiful children, Jackie and Paul, and knockout wife, the love of his life, who made a great living in the advertising business. Lisa and Simon saved enough by not paying rent at Sommerset House to finally be able to purchase their dream home in White Plains, New York. It was a far cry from his days in prison, and he wisely avoided a life with the wise guys in Detroit and the Bronx.

"Things were going great in our lives when suddenly, I began to notice little things that Lisa was forgetting. She seemed confused in the morning when she made coffee. When she dressed, it began taking her much longer than usual. It seemed that details of everyday life were forgotten, and she looked slightly lost at times. I watched this for a while until I thought I needed to look into things further," Simon recalled.

Simon decided to take Lisa to lunch one day and arrived before noon at her office at Ogilvy Advertising in Manhattan on 46th Street and 11th Avenue. Simon made it his business to run into Lisa's boss in the office and asked her if she had noticed anything different about his wife. The answer he received made his heart sink. The woman motioned Simon into her office.

"Lisa's boss had noticed that something was drastically wrong with my wife. In fact, she told me she was about to call me. Tasks that would normally take Lisa thirty minutes to finish would take her several hours to complete, and it would be rife with errors. One error cost the agency over one million dollars. Her boss said they didn't want to fire Lisa because they all loved her at Ogilvy, as she had been such a loyal and expert employee. The boss recommended I take Lisa to a doctor. My world was turned around by that conversation. I was devastated, to say the least."

That day, Simon took Lisa to Sam's Place, a small restaurant owned by his dear friend, Massimo, on Lexington Avenue and 39th Street.

"I gently asked my darling wife how she was doing. I mentioned that something may be wrong with her memory. Lisa immediately agreed—she knew she was having a problem with her memory. We thought perhaps it was menopause or just that things were catching up on her with her busy work and home schedule. I think we were in denial or just hoping against hope."

A visit to Lisa's doctor led to an appointment with a well-known neurologist on Park Avenue in Manhattan who put her through a bevy of tests. The results were earth shattering for the Qafa family.

Lisa was only forty-seven years old and diagnosed with early onset Alzheimer's disease. This disease has no cure, and at that moment, and even now, there is no help on the horizon.

Aside from the emotional devastation, there was the practical side of the disease. What about her job? What about Simon's position? What about long-term care for Lisa? What about their children? How long would this last? A million questions shouted out at Simon.

Ogilvy was extremely generous to Lisa and the Qafa family. Lisa's boss had promised long-term, full disability and other accrued benefits that helped enormously until the day she passed.

After her diagnosis, Lisa was no longer permitted to drive. The entire family's lives were put on hold.

Soon after her diagnosis, Cardinal Angelo Comastri, Simon's spiritual advisor from his days in the seminary in Rome, learned of Lisa's condition. The cardinal called Simon from the Vatican and offered, then insisted, that Simon bring Lisa to the Vatican's world-renowned neurological hospitals in both Florence and Bologna, Italy.

Simon took his wife to both Vatican hospitals in Italy, and sadly, the diagnosis was fully confirmed. There was no hope, either for a cure or for remission. Each confirmation of the disease was like a blow to the stomach.

Simon had promised Lisa she would never be sent to a nursing home, no matter how bad her condition became. She had taken great solace in his words as she feared dying alone in a strange bed, in a strange place.

Simon left his job at Sommerset House to be Lisa's

nurse and caregiver, watching his beloved wife sink into the darkness of Alzheimer's, losing a bit of her mind day by torturous day. It seemed as if a slice of her brain was being taken bit by bit.

Early on, Lisa would become increasingly depressed and then aggressive. She realized what was happening to her and naturally had a hard time dealing with her disease. Lisa was frustrated more and more as the days progressed.

As time went by, beyond the memory loss, Lisa had problems with her balance and daily hygiene. Simon cared for her lovingly but had his moments of despair. He asked God, Why *Lisa?* Why would such a gentle, loving woman must endure this awful life that would take her away piece by piece, day by day? Simon never lost his faith. He never asked God, *why me?* Why Simon? His prayers were for Lisa and Paul and Jackie. He asked God for his children to be sustained during this ordeal.

The kids knew how hard their father was working on their mother's daily activities. Feeding her, bathing her, and supporting her in every way that was humanly possible.

As the years passed, Lisa began to fade slowly. From not being able to talk, to eventually being bedridden for the last two years of her life. But her smile never faded. She tried as hard as she could to make things tolerable for her family.

Jackie and Paul naturally became depressed, having to put their lives on hold and watch their mother fade away. Their father was also emotionally ravaged by this horrid disease. The kids encouraged their father to go out on Friday nights to see his friends at Dominick Restaurant in the Bronx, where he would have dinner with the guys and a few drinks at La Parisiane Cafe for a few hours and return with dinner for the family.

Alzheimer's took Lisa after a long eleven years of suffering. The doctors had predicted ten to fifteen years at the most.

In Simons words, "I watched her and held her hand at the end. It was like watching a bright candle flicker and finally burn out."

The end came mercifully for Lisa and her family.

When she died, Lisa left a void in the lives of everyone who knew her. She was beautiful, charming, bright, and loving. The legacy she left was her two wonderful children and a husband who loved her unconditionally.

At her wake, in White Plains, New York, during the Covid-19 pandemic, when people were not even going out of their homes for fear of catching the virus, hundreds and hundreds of mourners walked past her casket, viewing a ravaged shell that was once their beautiful friend or family member. They came from as far away as California, Michigan, Florida, and New Jersey to pay their last respects. The family was greatly comforted by this outpouring of support.

The line of cars and the hundreds of people at the burial site at Gates of Heaven Cemetery in Hawthorne, New York were a small part of the testament of respect and love that was shown to the Qafa family.

CHAPTER SIXTEEN

Not every story about Pjeter Çup Qafa is about fighting the dreaded Sigurimi or the Albanian Communist Army in the hills and mountains. Not every story is about life and death struggles, even though the insurgents were constantly surrounded by their enemies. Some stories are simply humorous and entertaining.

Within these lighthearted tales, there is always the underlying lesson of survival and deep-rooted Albanian cultural nuances.

Simon Qafa recalls a story of his father, Pjeter Çup Qafa, from when he was ten years old. The family was living in Kosovo. Simon doesn't recall exactly where they were living as they were forced to move to six different towns in their time as refugees in Kosovo. The Albanians were not permitted to spread their roots and truly settle down.

"We were walking to visit friends who lived about three kilometers away. While we were traveling, I spotted a plump rabbit standing upright on its thick back legs. Meat was extremely scarce, and we were all quite hungry. Hunger was a constant in our lives. I pointed the hare out to my father. 'Dad, look at the size of that rabbit. Shoot him, and we can get some good meat for the family,' I said. My dad had one excuse after another as to why he couldn't shoot the cottontail. 'He's too far away, the wind is too strong for me to hit him, I can't hit him from this angle.'

"Now, you must remember that my father was an expert marksman, and I knew with absolute certainly that the rabbit had no chance. Dad made a noise, and the nervous hare fled into the brush. I was upset with my father for quite some time. We needed that meat urgently. Frankly, I was unhappy with my dad for months.

"Some thirty years later, we were reminiscing about the old days while the family was living in Detroit. I brought up the rabbit story. 'You know, Dad, that I was upset with you for the longest time. I still to this day don't know why you didn't shoot the animal when we were so hungry."

Pjeter replied, "I know you were angry. How could I have explained to you the real reason when you were ten years old? You see, I only had one bullet left in my gun."

Simon protested, "You were an expert with the gun. The rabbit had no chance to escape."

"If I missed or killed the rabbit, the result was the same. You see, my son, I needed that bullet. If we were suddenly overtaken by the Sigurimi, I had no way to kill myself. I had vowed never to let those bastards take me alive. Do you remember that soon after that day I went into the mountains with plenty of ammunition and came back with three rabbits? Your young memory is just of that fat rabbit that got away. I took twenty bullets with me and came back with seventeen," Pjeter explained.

Pjeter's overriding thought was to end his life in case he was apprehended rather than feed his family at that moment. This is the kind of desperation the communists had brought upon the hero of the mountains.

Another story of danger and desperation ended in a positive, almost funny result.

Pjeter had received word from friends that his nephew on his father's side had been approached by the Sigurimi. The nephew was promised a new suit if he would cooperate and give information on when and where Pjeter Qafa was returning to Albania.

Simon recalled the story which he heard from his father. "A suit of clothes was a big deal back then. It was prestigious to wear a new suit. There was no way anyone could afford such a luxury. This stupid guy decided to sell a blood relative for clothing. My father was furious, so he left Kosovo to confront this misguided nephew."

Pjeter Qafa approached the house where the nephew was living. He hid himself in the brush in the early morning waiting for dawn. The bathroom, like almost every house in the region back then, was in the rear of the house.

Pjeter knew that the nephew would eventually have to use the bathroom. Sure enough, at around six a.m. when the sun was up, the nephew made his way to the outhouse to relieve himself.

Simon tells the rest of the story. "When the nephew

came to the door of the bathroom, my father snuck behind him, putting the barrel of his rifle into the traitor's ribs. 'Good morning. Are you the one willing to betray me to the Sigurimi for a suit of clothes?' The nephew turned to see that it was Pjeter Çup Qafa, and he immediately pissed his pants. My father then made him a promise. 'Listen carefully to my words, nephew. If I find out that you have cooperated with these dogs, now or anytime in the future, I will return in the dark of night. I will find you and skin you alive with a Gillette. He smashed the hapless nephew on his head with the butt of his rifle and kicked him in the balls when he was on the ground. My father told him, 'Now tell those fucking Sigurimi that you don't need their fucking suit, if you know what's good for you.'"

It was bad enough that the Sigurimi and the Albanian communist army were pursuing Pjeter Qafa to torture and kill him. Qafa had to worry about a treacherous family member who was willing to turn on him. Desperate men make desperate moves. The wretched nephew saw the error of his ways and kept his skin intact.

Another story of near disaster which turned into comedy befell Pjeter Qafa.

On one of his sojourns from Albania back to Kosovo, Pjeter Qafa had planned to visit a kumar near Kukse. He had to traverse the Drin River to get to his destination. Spanning 177 miles, the

Drin was the longest river in Albania.

The day and night before he arrived at the Drin, there was a massive rainfall that caused the river to swell and trees to fall.

Pjeter was determined to swim across the wide river that had a depth of about twenty feet. Carrying a machine gun latched across his chest, two pistols, two homemade hand grenade bombs, and a bag of supplies on his back, the fully clothed Pjeter Qafa waded into the river. As he began to swim, a massive tree came rushing down the river upon him. The tree dragged the unsuspecting Qafa under the water. He fought hard to extract himself from the floating tree as its girth was getting the best of him. After his life-and-death battle with the tree, and after nearly drowning, Pjeter Qafa finally popped up to the surface of the Drin. When he reached the other side of the river, the only thing he had left on his body was the machine gun strapped to his chest. Lost were all his clothing, the bombs, his boots, and his pistols. Qafa was buck naked.

He made his way to the home of Hazhi Fetahi, his kumar, and great grandfather of Abdullah Nezaj. It was ten o'clock in the morning, and Pjeter Qafa had wrapped himself in parts of shrubbery to hide his nakedness.

Qafa noticed a single light coming from the interior of the house. He surmised the light was coming from the room that only men would sit in as was the Albanian tradition in that region. Qafa knocked on the door while holding the bush parts around his lower parts.

Hazhi peered out of his window and went to the door.

"Kumar, tell me it is you and not the devil at my

door," Hazhi blurted. Both
men laughed heartily at Pjeter's condition.

Qafa had to find some pants and shirt to wear before he resumed traveling the next morning.

Hazhi found a pair of his grandson's pants. Tall like his son, Abdulla Nezaj, the pants were way too long for the shorter Pjeter Qafa.

"How the hell can I wear these trousers? Look how long they are. I will be dragging them through the mountains," Qafa laughed.

"Roll them up or put the bushes back on to cover you," Hazhi replied.

It was no accident that the only thing Pjeter Qafa came away from the Drin River with was his machine gun. Guns were sacrosanct among the men who made their commitment to evade the communists and save the lives of their countrymen.

CHAPTER SEVENTEEN

On another dinner meeting at Dominick's in the Bronx and coffee and drinks at Le Parisian Café with Abdullah Nezaj, Tony Vuksanaj, and Simon Qafa, I asked a pointed question.

I suppose my question was naïve due to my lack of cultural understanding, and perhaps over the line, but I asked it anyway.

"Were there any stories of men who were taking widows with children across the border to Kosovo where they would have relations with the women? After all, men are men, and human nature is what it is," I asked.

Simon and Abdullah responded without pausing.

Simon spoke first. "These men looked upon these women as their sisters. They didn't have a remote feeling about having sex with them. Mothers and their children were their highest priority. All the men took vows to protect these women."

Abdullah jumped in. "If they were to do such a thing, they would be denigrated to the lowest creature. You must remember, these men were the best of the best of the Albanians."

Simon recalled a story that Pjeter Çup Qafa had spoken about. "One time my father had to sneak down into a house. He lowered himself into the bedroom of the home and saw that the woman of the house was sleeping naked on top of the bed. The husband was out of the house. My dad averted his eyes and quietly covered the woman with a blanket. He would not even gape at the naked lady, even though he was in the mountains for some time. Many years later, after the death of my father, this woman was at our home in Detroit. She asked if my father ever told them that he saw her naked in her bed. She realized someone covered her and knew that Pjeter was in the house. Our answer was that my father never mentioned it. She was relieved that her modesty was intact. These are the kind of men we are talking about."

"These men must have suffered many hardships in the mountains," I said.

Abdullah added, "Yes, everyone did. Getting fresh water and avoiding dehydration was a big challenge. Often, after it rained, we would drink the water that puddled into the footprints of horses. We survived any way we could. I remember going to a well and bringing up a bucket of water. Before we could drink, we had to brush off bird shit and other waste from the top of the water. We all drank directly from streams and rivers whenever we were near them. Somehow, no one got sick from the water. It wasn't like today where you can go to a store and buy bottles of water. That didn't exist in our world."

Pjeter Çup Qafa Random Stories

Earned respect is one of the vital attributes an Albanian man can seek. In Pjeter Çup Qafa's life, he earned much esteem among the Albanians, Kosovans, and, for that matter, all the Balkans. It is often asked of powerful people whether they would rather be loved or feared, and the debate has excellent arguments on both sides. Pjeter Çup Qafa was a unique man who was able to achieve both love and fear during his lifetime and beyond.

Some of the stories of his life in Albania, Kosovo, and the United States illustrate the respect and power that Pjeter wielded among not only his peers but among his enemies as well.

Pjeter was often called upon to settle blood disputes, marital arguments, and land feuds. Among the Albanians, it is easier to settle a blood feud over someone that was killed than a feud over someone who was beaten. Beating a man was a disgrace against the family that was beyond what western cultures would deem as a simple embarrassment.

Vengeance on a beating was worse than the retribution on a killing. Often, a killing was able to be justified by its cause. Mitigating circumstances would at times be considered. If a man was killed for a crime against another family, often the offended family could be reasoned with. The result of a man being disgraced by a beating was not so easy to mediate.

The UDB, the Yugoslavian communist government's answer to the American CIA did nothing to thwart Gjakmarrja, the blood vengeance among the Albanians. The reasons were clear. The government didn't want peace and would rather see Albanians kill each other.

***

Pjeter was called to the village of Gjurakoc in the municipality of Istog, Kosovo. Pjeter was asked to intervene in a land dispute between two brothers. He walked for over four hours in the heat of the day, alone, on hard-pan paths as it had not rained in some time. None of the paths would be considered roads. The only means of traveling this path were by foot or horse. No vehicle could traverse the rough terrain.

When Pjeter arrived in Gjurakoc, he assessed the situation. He was there to intervene before the brothers, whom he knew had come to blows. They each had an ax they were ready to use on each other over a small land parcel of fifty meters.

Pjeter sat with the brothers who respected him enough to keep their bitterness calm for the moment.

Pjeter listened to each brother without commenting. When the talking ended, Pjeter called over a ten-year-old boy standing nearby with a younger cousin.

"Son, I want you and your cousin to go over into that field and bring me back ten stones as big as your heads," Pjeter ordered. Within minutes, the boys returned with their arms filled with stones from the barren field.

Pjeter got down low, surveying the property by eye. He asked for a shovel and told the boys to walk with him. With the shovel, Pjeter opened a hole in the ground. He ordered the older boy to drop a stone into the hole, so the top of the stone showed above the surface. Pjeter walked about ten yards and repeated the process—hole, then rock. This was done until all the rocks were placed. The property was divided equally in half.

Pjeter tossed the shovel away and addressed the two brothers in a calm, quiet voice.

"There. Your property is now divided. These rocks are the Pjeter Çup Qafa boarder. If I hear that you are disputing my judgement, I will return and kill both of your dumb asses."

To this day, the boarder has stood.

Years later, when a road was proposed to go through the property, the two brothers convinced them that it be built around the Pjeter Çup Qafa boarder.

***

Another story of Pjeter's intervention, this time regarding a marriage, became legend.

In the early 1960's, a distant cousin of the Qafas married a girl from the village of Bistazhin.

The day after the wedding night, the groom sent the bride back to her parents. He claimed she was not a virgin when he married her. A virgin bride is the only way a man would accept a woman in that culture at that time.

The bride and her mother adamantly denied the groom's allegation. Tempers began to flare, and nothing good would have come as a result. The situation was becoming dangerous as the men were becoming involved in the dispute. Pjeter Çup Qafa was sent for from the village of Budisalc which was a distance by foot of three to four hours.

Pjeter took the journey and arrived at his cousin's home, immediately sending for the bride's father. They sat in the one-room house at a handmade wooden table with six chairs, all made by relatives of the Qafas generations before.

Coffee was served, and pleasant discussion about the weather and farming were passed around until it was time to get to business. After all, this man was a guest in their home and deserved respect as the Kunan demands.

"How are we going to settle this?" Pjeter asked.

The bride's father, who was furious at the idea of his daughter's reputation being destroyed, tempered his anger in the presence of Pjeter and demanded that his wife and daughter be summoned to defend her honor.

The groom, Pjeter's distant cousin, stated emphatically that the bride had admitted to him she had an affair before they married.

The bride and her mother arrived, and Pjeter Çup

Qafa immediately took out his handgun and slammed it on the table.

"No way will a woman come and sit in my presence. I will put a stop to this dispute now. This case is closed. The girl returns to her mother. There is no marriage. Now, if there is any further dispute on this matter, I will return here, but I will not come alone. You all know what that means."

The bride's father had no choice but to agree to the terms.

Pjeter immediately returned home, walking a total of eight hours in one day.

The marriage was annulled.

***

Not every story about Pjeter Çup Qafa is filled with drama. Some are comical.

In one village, word was passed around that the legend of the mountains would be walking through on a particular day.

Six women in the village were lined up along an old, rickety, wooden fence to catch a glimpse of Pjeter.

Standing along the fence in their traditional long dresses and head scarfs, the women saw Pjeter walking their way. As the women pressed to get a better look, they leaned against the fence. The rotted posts gave way, collapsing the fence and sending the ladies sprawling to the ground.

Pjeter laughed until he almost doubled over.

"If you ladies wanted to see me and say hello, I

would have walked into your yards," Pjeter laughed.

He could tell the women were nervous their husbands would hear of the incident and be angry and punish them.

"Let's all walk to the square and see your husbands," Pjeter stated.

Reluctantly, the women led the way to their husbands, and Pjeter approached the men while they were smoking cigarettes and chatting.

"Good day, gentlemen. These women were anxious to say hello to me. They are all good women, and the fence they were leaning on needs repair. I say to you that they are all under my Besa. They are not to be touched or punished in any way," Pjeter announced.

The men all agreed, and they laughed at the innocent incident.

This was how things were in those days, and Pjeter Çup Qafa's word was enough to save the women from their husbands' wrath.

***

Another quasi-comical story was the time that Pjeter decided to dress like a Sigurimi general to go visit friends of his in Albania. Along the route, an army captain and ten of his men came upon

Pjeter in a clearing. Pjeter had come out of the protection of some trees and was caught unaware.

"Halt. What is the password?" the captain called out to Pjeter.

"The password? Where do you get the balls to ask

me for the password? Don't you see my uniform, you idiot?" Pjeter yelled.

He approached the captain, dressing him down in front of his men. The captain hung his head while Pjeter was hollering at him. In dramatic fashion, Pjeter walked up to the captain and lifted his head from under his chin.

"Look at me when I speak to you, captain, and bring your men to attention."

The captain complied.

"Now, I want you and your men to button up their uniforms to look like real soldiers. Then every one of you will doone hundred pushups."

The group began the sit ups, and Pjeter Qafa calmly walked back to the safety of the forest.

***

In those days, corporal punishment was often issued to women by their husbands. It was part of their culture going back hundreds of years.

Simon Qafa told a story of his esteemed father also using his hands to reprimand his wife.

When Simon was ten years old, he witnessed his father hitting his mother for some menial infraction.

"I approached my father with anger and grabbed his hand. I told him if he ever hit my mother again, I would kill him. My father was proud of my defending my mom and he never laid hands on her again," Simon remembered.

***

Names of the family in this story cannot be mentioned as the family is still prominent in the Albanian community.

In Detroit, a young woman was about to be married. In fact, her wedding day was tomorrow. Instead, she eloped with her lover, and they ran away to New York City for a few days.

Her distraught and embarrassed fiancé went to see Pjeter Çup Qafa.

"You know why I came, Pjeter," the fiancé said.

"Yes, I do. It's probably for the best," Pjeter replied.

"You are well known for settling these kinds of matters. I want to ask you: What would you do if you were in my position?"

Pjeter thought for a while and finally gave his answer.

"Here is what I would do in your case. Take some raki and some sugar. Go to the in-laws and forgive them and go on about your life. Or shoot them," Pjeter offered. The advice about shooting them was a joke, sort of a tongue-in-cheek remark.

A few weeks later, on a Sunday, the bride and her family went to mass. There was no Albanian church at that time in Detroit, so they went to a Catholic church on Miller Street that was friendly to the Albanian community.

As the family left the church, the jilted man's ex-fiancé and her husband were together on Miller Street. The jilted man took Pjeter Qafa's advice, stepped out of his car, and opened fire on the couple. He shot up their car and left the bride with a prominent scar on her face with a near fatal bullet.

Word spread through the community that Pjeter Qafa had advised the man to shoot his former fiancé and her man. Her family now accused Pjeter.

Without hesitation, Pjeter went to see the family. By the time he left them, their accusations had turned into apologies.

Simon Qafa

Simon Qafa has continued his fight against communism and socialism in the United States and Europe, even now in 2022.

Unlike his father, Pjeter Qafa the legend of the mountains, Simon is not using machine guns, pistols, and handmade bombs to combat the enemy. He uses Facebook as his pulpit to let people know of the insidious communist theories that are being forced upon the American people by a corrupt mainstream media and a "progressive" Democrat party.

Simon is an avid user of the social media platform that Facebook has developed to inform anyone who is willing to listen about the direction the world is going in. He informs the public of the communists not only in Albania, but also within the Unites States government.

Unfortunately, Facebook has become part of the left-wing conspiracy to stifle conservative thinking. Many of Simon's posts are either edited by Facebook, or he is thrown into Facebook "jail" for his thinking.

Facebook has used their "jail" to keep Simon from posting against the Democrats who are insisting on a socialist agenda. He has been jailed countless times, usually getting blocked from posting for thirty days at a time. Simon has combatted this censorship by having numerous accounts under various names to keep his ideas flowing to his many followers. He continues his fight on a daily basis as his ancestors did for centuries. Not with bullets and bombs, but with words, which in the opinion of the left are more dangerous than conventional war weapons.

Simon posts ten or more messages a day on Facebook. Each one has a lesson and occasionally a joke that also teaches. Here are just a few of Simon's posts, some of which have been reported to Facebook by left-wing sympathizers and detractors of Simon's message.

Remember when Putin was supposed to commit suicide, or his generals were going to kill him within a couple of weeks?

Remember when sanctions were going to choke him? Well guess who's paying $6 a gallon, certainly not Russians.

And now Putin is making billions each day from China, India and Pakistan, while we DON'T have baby formula for our kids.

Who from you remembers when I wrote the sanction were going to hurt American people more than Putin?

Since we are going after Oligarch why aren't we confiscating Hunter BIDEN'S millions that he accumulated from Oligarch?

Enjoy ur grass. DON'T forget salt and pepper.

"The deadliest sin in the world today, is the killing of unborn children"
- Saint Mother Teresa.
Now that's how a true Christian talks and feels.
All the others are fake Christians. I'm sure not one of you can be more forgiving than Saint Mother Teresa, but there are evil things out there that cannot be forgiven!

I tell you something.
It takes a very special kind of stupid to ruin the greatest country in the world within 16 months.
Watch out, this special kind of stupid is coming for you next!
To all you good people out ther who are tired of reading my zillion posts an hour, tell your scumbag friends not to snitch on me and get banned for 30 days. Because when I come back, I come back with a vengeance. As you can see.

Liberals should thank and buy Rolexes for the conservative justices who overturned Roe vs Wade.

Because of them, no one is talking about inflation, gas prices, empty shelves, Russia and Ukraine, the Afghanistan disaster, Alec Baldwin, Hunter Biden, 46 dead illegals, murders and crimes in general …

I'm not sure these justices are not working with liberals under the table

Am I right or am I right?

There are 3 kinds of idiots out there:
The ones who believe everything is Putin's fault
The ones who believe anything Biden says
The ones who watch The View

WDIV DETROIT
Has banned me from commenting on their posts.

Since I can't comment, then I will share your posts and tell 5,000 of my friends around the world how butt hurt you are!

These deaths are squarely on this administration's hands.

Block that, you b*tches.

I need a good lawyer to defend me against Zuckerberg's harassment. Peter Lumaj, Ylli Cekani, Fatos Dervishi. Cka, sju pelqejn JU paret e mija counterfeit.

Biden promised to enhance our forces in Europe ... kinda like he did in Afghanistan, leaving some $86 billion dollar's worth of American Arms to Taliban and Al Qaeda?

He got jokes, this clown.

Why are the NY governor and our mayor and democrats in general so pro criminals and anti law-abiding citizens?

Since when do criminals need a gun license to carry a gun for their crimes?

By protesting the SCOTUS gun decision, you are telling a rapist, go rape that woman, she DON'T have a gun.

You are telling a robber, go rob that person, he's not allowed to carry a gun, and so on.

Imagine a drug cartel leader asking for a gun permit?

Imagine a MS-13 thug asking for a gun permit?

It is beyond my comprehension why democrats love to take the side of criminals!

Let the law-abiding citizens protect themselves, their families, and their properties legally since the police can't do it any longer due to attacks on our law enforcement!

She lied under oath.
Why aren't REPUBLICANS on the steps of Capitol Hill 24/7 in front of cameras like Pelosi, Schumer, and Schiff do when democrats want to make a point.
Grow some balls, you spineless despicable idiots!

Jan 6 Committee owes Trump an apology for this farce of testimony. And she should go to jail for lying under oath!
Is this Russian Collusion 2.0?
Nobody seems to go to jail for lying under oath as long as they lie against Trump.

When Republicans get back Senate and Congress in November, I promise I will be very gentle with the feelings of cry babies out there.

Fact:
Liberals are anti human and anti humanity unless of course it fits their narrative.

Did you see any liberal at the steps of the Capitol mourning 46 illegals who died like animals locked up in a trailer truck?

Kinda like you don't see them mourn innocent victims of Chicago, LA, Philadelphia, Baltimore, NY, DC etc....

In a relationship!!

She's from Cuba and her name is COHIBA

Dear Catholics out there:
Stop fooling yourself because you can't fool God.

If you are pro-abortion, your faith is a shaky one at best.

Where have you read in the Bible, Gospel, or the Acts of Apostles where it says it's ok to kill God's children?

I can cite you numerous places where Jesus says "DON'T hurt the children of God. Let the children come to me."

To all these Liberals who are elected officials, who are threatening, cursing, and using profanities against SCOTUS justices:

YOU ARE DOMESTIC TERRORISTS!

You are mad because Trump single handedly reversed Roe v Wade.

SOME RANDOM SIMON STORIES

Simon Qafa has been a big promotor and proponent of the author's books.

When I wrote my best-selling book BESA, a novel about a fictitious Albanian crime family and the New York Italian mob, Simon was influential in getting an interview with me on Albanian television as well as a few book signing events. He was also in a four-minute teaser reel for BESA that I produced. Simon was the only non-Screen Actors Guild (SAG) actor in the piece. Simon has a great camera presence and I have a feeling he could have been an excellent actor if he chose that path.

Simon set up a book signing at St. Paul Albanian Catholic Church in Detroit for me and BESA. Simon and I flew to Detroit from New York City. The large Albanian community in Detroit welcomed me with open arms.

The huge community room at St. Paul's had paintings of Pope John Paul and Pope Benedict XVI on the walls as well a magnificent painting of Gjergi Kastrioti. A large beautiful Albanian flag hung on a wall near Skanderbeg's image. That's where our event took place.

I signed over one hundred BESA books, taking photos and shaking hands with the parishioners. I had a great time and met many wonderful people. I wound up donating the books and the proceeds to St. Paul's. I was delighted to do this for this wonderful parish.

During the signing, I witnessed a very attractive woman, with two small children in tow invite herself to join Simon in the hotel where we were staying. Charisma and good looks could be a blessing and a curse at the same time. I was floored that this would happen on church grounds being educated in Catholic schools myself. Simon made it clear that he was married, and this assignation was not to be.

We were scheduled to fly from Detroit to LaGuardia airport the next day. It is said that man plans, and God laughs and that was true on this trip.

Superstorm Sandy hit the United States hard and all air flights were cancelled. I needed to get back to New York as did Simon. The only way out of Detroit was to rent a car for the eleven-hour trek. Simon volunteered to drive the entire way and two Albanian speaking writers hitched a ride with us.

Most of the ride was in heavy rain but we chatted, and the time passed. I heard every word in Albanian that our riders talked and understood nothing, but the ride was uneventful. That was, until we got to the New Jersey boarder.

The scene was out of a movie. The weather was so severe that we could hardly see out the windshield. It seemed that the eye of the Storm was following us the minute we saw the Welcome to New Jersey sign.

The roads were beginning to flood and trees and electricity poles were falling everywhere. Simon maneuvered the car, a big Ford sedan around the flooded roads and felled timber. It seemed the car had wings as the rainwater sprayed from the front tires.

The night was totally black. Electric capacitors were exploding all around us. It looked like the old movie "War of the Worlds." The only thing missing were the invading Martians. Simon kept cool. My stomach was in knots. The Albanians in the back seat went very quiet.

Now we had to weave our way up to North Jersey where I live. The roads were worsening by the minute. An announcement on the radio informed us the bridges over the Hudson River were already closed or soon closing due to high winds. Problem was, Simon lived in White Plains, New York and our passengers lived in nearby Connecticut.

We began calling the bridges. The Tappan Zee was closed in both directions as was the George Washington Bridge. I invited Simon and the others to stay at my home and wait for Sandy to pass. Simon said, "I am going home to see my wife and kids and sleep in my bed." That settled that.

I called the Bear Mountain Bridge.

Miraculously they were open but planning to close in two hours. There was just enough time for Simon to make the deadline.

I told Simon to drop me off at a hotel in Mahwah, New Jersey right off highway 287. I called ahead and my son Daniel would pick me up and Simon could remain on the highway. I live ten minutes from the Sheraton

Crossroads Hotel. The ride took nearly an hour because of the flooded roads and felled trees.

Simon just made it before the Bear Mountain Bridge closed. He drove the two writers to Connecticut and made it home to see his family after one the next morning.

When Simon Qafa puts something in his head, no one can change it.

***

Simon's reputation precedes him just as his father Pjeter Qup Qafa's status put fear into some.

Since Simon shot the brothers in Brooklyn, over forty years later there are people in the community that still think he still is a stone-cold killer. One family who will remain nameless had a relative shot dead within the last ten years. The police were unable to apprehend the killer. The family thought Simon Qafa was the shooter because the murder victim's family was part of the planning of the assassination of the Qafa Kumar so many years ago. The police summoned Simon for questioning. His alibi was iron clad. Simon was nowhere near the scene. It was later discovered that the man was shot dead due to a private blood feud unrelated to the Kumar's murder.

***

A kind of cute story that Simon talks about when he was remanded to Dannemora prison. When he arrived at Clinton the first thing the prison administration did was shave the prisoners' heads.

When his family was able to visit, which was not an easy trip from Detroit to Clinton County in upstate New York, Simon's mother Liza and his father Pjeter and Dom Preka met with the prisoner who was behind a screened in area. Of course, Pjeter Qafa, being strong and fearless took seeing Simon in stride. They were all just happy to see Simon Liza Qafa was not so strong. She started crying immediately. When she was able to gather herself, Simon tried to comfort her, "Mom, I'll be out in two years. It's nothing. It will go by fast." To which Liza Qafa replied, "I'm not crying for the time. Look what they did to your hair!"

KUJTIM

August 1951, after being in political exile in Kosovo for two years, the Qafa family welcomed an addition, the birth of Pjeter Qafas first son Kujtim. After the baptism the little boy was named Gjon (John) by his famous freedom fighter Godfather, Gjon Gjinaj.

The news spread around quickly among Pjeter's anti-communist friends who were also in exile in Kosovo. They decided one Sunday to come and visit the Qafas and congratulate them on the addition to the family. After a few songs and raki shots, they asked Pjeter if they could give his son a new name, since he was the first child born in exile and Pjeter with no hesitation told them to go ahead. They named him Kujtim a fitting name which in English means remembrance. And to this day he's officially known as Kujtim and not John.

When the Qafa family emigrated to US in 1968, they settled in Stamford Connecticut and young Kujtim found a job in construction to help his parents with expenses and payback the debt they had incurred while waiting in San Biagio to be granted political asylum by the U.S.

In 1973, the family moved to Detroit and resided in Dane street. The Albanian community took a liking to young Kujtim inviting him to participate in meetings, demonstrations, and other activities. During these demonstrations against communism and against the injustices the Yugoslavian government, which was inflicted on the Albanians in Kosovo, Kujtim became a well-known leader of the cause.

Kujtim met with many senators, congressman, and a few presidents, namely Reagan, Clinton, and Bush which he took as a great honor.

Kujtim also formed the Detroit BESA Soccer Club. The team played locally and after a few years, moved up to the Canadian semi-pro league.

Kujtim opened a fast-food restaurant in Detroit and made an excellent living for his family. Political participations were very costly, but Kujtim spared no expenses when it came to his beloved country.

He traveled from Detroit to Lubljana, capital of Slovenia and met with General Tom Berisha and commander Naim Maloku, to help create UÇK (Kosova Liberation Army) to confront the brutal Yugoslavian army. Kujtim handed them $5,000, a large amount at that time to help buy arms.

Kujtim has been decorated by the Michigan Albanian community and by the Albanian-American Federation VATRA in NY.

With these heavy expenses and acquiring an appetite for gambling, Kujtim's fortunes were on the wane. He divorced and filed for bankruptcy.

Few years ago, Kujtim, had a stroke that left him half paralyzed. He spends his days now at his house in a Detroit suburb. Occasionally his family and friends pick him up for a visit or dinners at local restaurants.

Kujtim is banned from driving in his condition.

Simon said of his older brother. "I salute my older brother for everything he has done for the family, friends, diaspora and for our Country."

THE FUTURE

I had the pleasure of interviewing Jackie Qafa, the eldest child of Simon and Lisa.

Here is a young woman, (32) who is well grounded, bright, articulate and as strong a personality as I have known. She has the warmth of intellect of her mother and the determination and focus of her father. With all these attributes Jackie is gifted in so many ways.

"I knew from a young girl my dad was well respected anywhere we went. Everyone seemed to know him in the Albanian community and showed deference and respect to him and to us. People told me he was a good guy and an important man. It made me feel great and sort of like a celebrity. I always thought it was because of my grandfather's reputation, which was certainly true, but I didn't know until I was much older what my father did for his family," Jackie explained.

Pjeter Çup Qafa passed away before Jackie could meet him. "I didn't meet my grandfather, but I feel as if I knew him my whole life. To learn about his greatness and bravery so many times, and to hear the stories about his life from so many people I have a feeling his spirit is still around us. I did know my grandmother, however. She was a tough lady and a saint."

"What do you mean by saint Jackie," I asked.

"She raises eight children and did it mostly alone because her husband was always away in his life as a freedom fighter. I remember her when I was a little girl, and we would go visit the family in Detroit. She had a tough exterior but was very good hearted. She was always giving us money even though she really had none."

I asked, "Tell me how you feel about Simon."

"I love him with all my heart and soul. I can tell you a carry a lot of his traits. He was so devoted to my mom and cared for when she was ill totally. There was no way mom was going into a nursing home and it was very tough on all of us. I learned a lot from my dad about love and loyalty during those terrible years my mom was so ill," Jackie responded.

"Do you share your father's passion for politics?" I inquired.

Jackie answered. "Honestly, I don't have much trust for politicians on both sides. Maybe part of my DNA would one day force me to get more vocal but at he moment I don't see much hope for positive change, but perhaps it will turn itself around."

"Jackie, tell me what's it's like being the daughter of Simon Qafa right now?"

Jackie laughed. "One night I was with friends in a bar and this guy found out what I was drinking and came to meet me. He placed my drink and his drink in front of me. He was obviously Albanian. Let's say his name was Zef, I've forgotten it. He introduced himself and asked for my name. 'I'm Jackie," I said. 'What is your last name?' He asked. 'Qafa', I replied. 'Tell me are you related to Simon Qafa', he asked. 'Yes, he's my father.' Zef stood up, took the two drinks and said, 'I can't go with you. I won't risk messing with Simon Qafa'. That about explains it."

***

I asked Paul Qafa about what his earliest memories of his father were. Like Jackie he did not know his grandfather Pjeter Çup Qafa, the legend of the mountains but grew up hearing all the oral history of his fearless family.

"I remember as a young boy my dad was a wholesome American father who would do anything for his family. He was the best dad ever. Always there for us and he still is. Dad always took me to soccer practices telling me how and where I could improve. Everyone we met always had the most respect for Simon. I didn't really understand why until I heard some stories when I got older and realized the tough guys he knew, and his history were the reasons why he was so respected and revered. It was a little more than my dad just being a nice guy."

"What do you know of your grandfather Pjeter Qafa?"

"I heard all of the stories. I knew he was an honorable man who brought many people from communism to freedom. I always felt an alure to my grandfather and would have loved to be like him."

"Are you into politics Paulie?" I asked.

"I am totally against socialism, and I detest communism. I guess that's in my blood. I remember in high school; some kids were wearing hammer and sickle tee-shirts and I didn't hold my tongue. They had no idea the horror so many people went through under the commies. It got very heated at times with me."

"Do you see yourself in politics?"

"No really at this point. I was never good in school, so I went to trade school and have done very well. I've always worked hard and will carry this work ethic all my life. I dislike the corruption in politics, and I could never be part of that kind of world."

"Tell me a couple of stories about your dad," I asked.

Paulie laughed out loud. "Sure. There was one time we were on vacation in Ocean Beach. I was playing soccer on the beach with my cousins and the ball hit into this guy who was lying on his blanket. We were little kids, and this guy gets up and goes crazy. He started screaming and yelling at us like a manic. Dad went over and said very nicely, we are just kids. Well, the guy made a mistake and pushed Simon. Dad proceeded to tool the guy up kicking his ass pretty good. When you're a kid and your dad is tough it's very impressionable."

"Do you have that fighting spirit Paulie?

"Well, I think I do. I remember when I was about five years old, we were somewhere, and this older kid started bothering Jackie. I guess he was about nine. My mother and aunts were there. I went over to the kid and punched him in the face a few times. That settled the matter. When dad found out he was pretty proud that I stepped up for my older sister."

"You must miss your mom," I queried.

"Every day. I have to say that I was seventeen when she got sick. The burden was more on Jackie and my dad, and I did everything I could to help them and ease their worry. I learned strength from my dad and my sister. Watching mom deteriorate for almost ten years and watching Jackie and Simon sacrifice their entire lives gave me a love and respect that can never waiver."

***

Throughout this book the common themes going back hundreds of years in the Qafa family history are fearlessness, love, determination, loyalty, respect, and faith. Knowing the character of Jackie and Paulie and their many cousins, the children of the Qafa clan will carry these inborn traits beyond the next millennium.

Pictures

BESA soccer team. Simon Qafa next to coach standing on left. 1977

Il Cardinal Angelo Comastri--Simon's mentor and father figure while at seminary in Rome.

III Cardinal Angelo Comastri--Simon's mentor and father figure while at seminary in Rome._2

IV Gjon Gjinaj King Zog's officers uniform 1939 in Shkodra, Albania.

V Gjon Gjinaj--Freedom fighter who parachuted twice in Albania fighting communists. Assassinated in NYC December 1977

VI

VII Kujtim Qafa

VIII Kujtim Qafa Albanian diaspora award in Detroit

IX Lisa and Simon Qafa with Cardinal Comastri in Vatican City 2013.

New York Eagles 1978
Back: ?, Andjelko Tesan, Van Taylor, Ron Hardy, ?, ?, Herve Guilbod, ?, Tom Mulroy, Hranislav Hadzitonic, Goalie?, Dragan Sekularac
Front: Pedro Molina, Ramon Mifflin, Simon Curanaj, Jeff Tipping, Simon Qafa, Clyde Brown, 8, Emir Travaljn, Clyde Watson

X New York Eagles Soccer team (American Soccer League). Simon Qafa fourth from left, kneeling.

XI Lisa Qafa 1982--the day Simon and Lisa met.

XII Lisa Qafa 2010

XIII Mark Gjomarkaj--Mirdita leader who organized the anti-communist movement. Killed fighting in 1946 in Mirdita.

XIV Nrec Nue Qafa, aka the Serbs worst nightmare.

XV Nrec Nue Qafa, aka the Serbs worst nightmare._2

XVI Nrec Nue Qafa, aka the Serbs worst nightmare._3

XVII Pal Qafa---Executed by communist firing squad in Albania 1975.

XVIII Paulie and Jackie Qafa

XIX Pjeter Çup Qafa

xx *Pjeter Çup Qafa playing the qiftelia*

XXI QAFA family

XXII Peter Cup Qafa--one man fighting machine. Known as the legend of the mountains._3

XXIII Peter Cup Qafa--one man fighting machine. Known as the legend of the mountains._4

XXIV Qafa family compound, called a Kulla.

XXV Qafa family flag

XXVI Simon Qafa in the mountains of Albania.

XXVII Simon Qafa the seminarian in Rome.

XXVIII Simon Qafa. BESA soccer team. 1977. Yugoslavia.

XXIX Simon walking in protest in Washington, D.C.

XXX Simon with author, Louis Romano.

XXXI Kujtim Qafa. Decorated by Albanian American Federation VATRA.

XXXII Simon's family

XXXIII Simon's fierce anti communist speeches.

XXXIV Simon's fierce anti communist speeches. _2

XXXV Simon Qafa fighting for American history. ANTIFA tried to topple Christopher Columbus statue in the Bronx

*Do you want to help the author get more recognition?
Please review this book!*

*Review via:
Goodreads.com
Or via your purchase platform!*

Acknowledgements

I will always remember the time I spent with Simon Qafa on this book commemorating the history of the Qafa family and his life.

Simon and I began a great friendship around the time I wrote BESA, and I fell in love with the Albanian people and their culture. I consider Simon my brother.

Thanks go out to Tony Vuksanaj, Abdulla Nezaj, and Sejdi Husenaj for their stories and input on the Qafa family.

It was an honor to interview Jackie and Paulie Qafa for their involvement and participation in this book.

The book cover was a brainchild of Simon Qafa and beautifully designed by Alison Lorenz.

A sincere thank you to Pauline Harris for her masterful editing.

Louis Romano

About the author:

Born in The Bronx, NY in 1950, Romano began his literary career in 2010 at age 60 after writing urban poetry since 18. He authored two poetry books, "Anxiety's Nest" and "Anxiety's Cure," which garnered a great response. He later penned a mob novel, "Fish Farm," followed by an award-winning screenplay and another mobster book, "BESA." Romano's recurring characters gained a dedicated readership. "GAME OF PAWNS" came out in 2016 and was a Pulitzer Prize contender, followed by "EXCLUSION: THE FIGHT FOR CHINATOWN" in 2018.

In 2012, he launched the Vic Gonnella Series, featuring Detective Vic Gonnella and Raquel Ruiz, starting with "INTERCESSION," an Amazon Best Seller. The series includes "JUSTIFIED," "YOU THINK I'M DEAD," "THE BUTCHER OF PUNTA CANA," "THE PIPELINE: Terror for New York," and "SHANDA," with "THE SURGEON" in progress.

Romano also authored a Teen/YA/Family series called "ZIP CODE," targeted at middle to high school students. His Heritage Collection Series began with "CARUSI: THE SHAME OF SICILY," followed by a collection of short stories titled "Things I Want to Tell You BEFORE I DROP DEAD."

In the True Crime genre, he wrote "John Alite: Mafia International" and the Amazon Best Seller "BORN IN THE LIFE" about mobster Gene Borrello. He added a novella, "IN THEIR FOOTSTEPS: QAFA FAMILY 300 YEARS OF WAR," to the Heritage Collection Series in 2023.

His latest work, co-authored with John Gjocaj in 2023, is "ON THE SIDE OF THE ROAD," along with "BESA" and "INTERCESSION," which are script-ready. For 2024, he has a new release titled "TRUST AND BETRAYAL: THE LEVIT FERNANDINI STORY," a True Crime book.

Romano resides in Northern New Jersey.

Sneak Peak of Intercession:

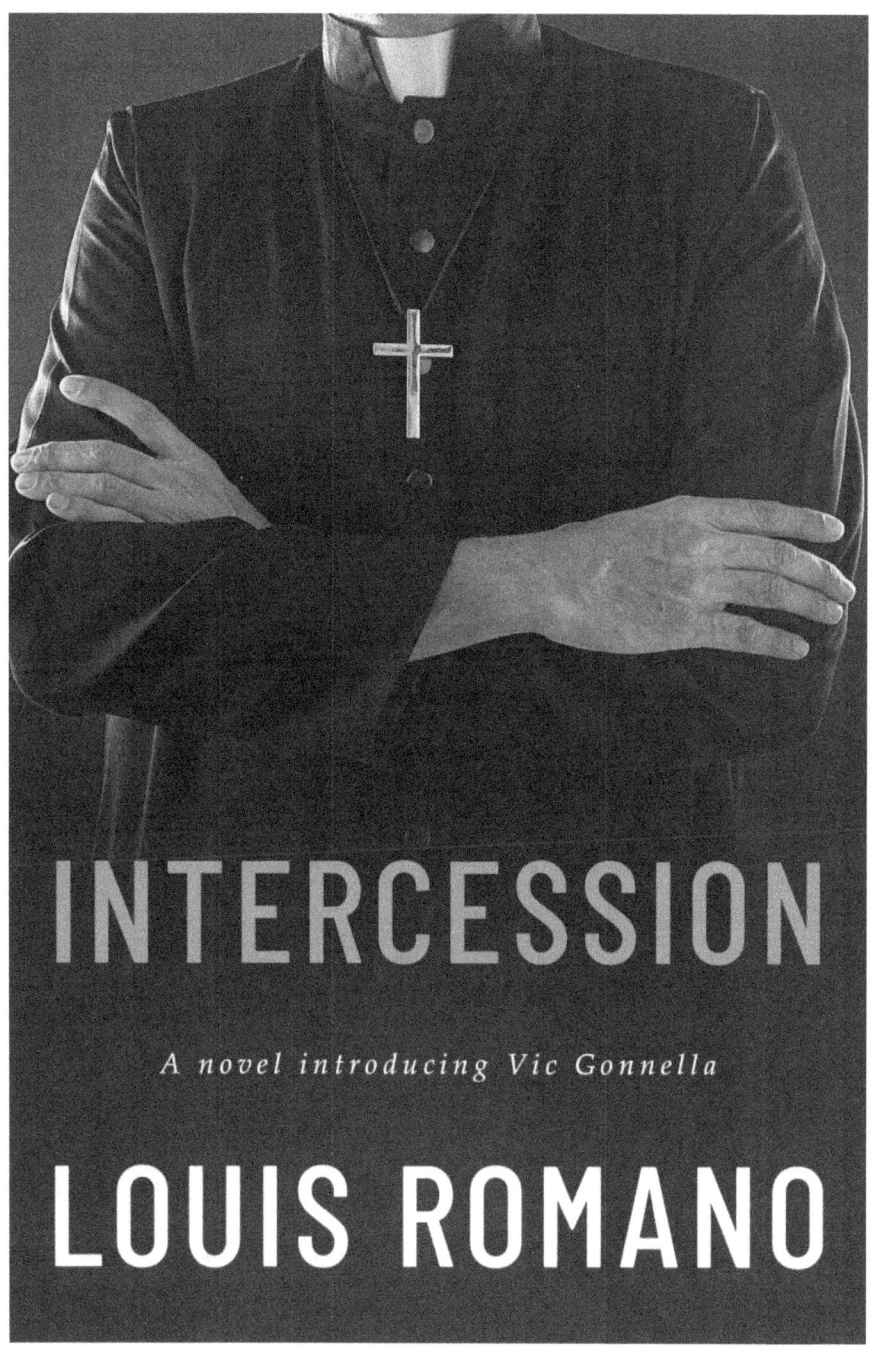

Chapter 1

2012, The Bronx, New York

There was a sharp rap on the door of the rectory at St. Martin of Tours Church. Father Edward O'Gorman tutted and looked at his watch. It was after 9 P.M., and visitors at that hour were not the norm. The church wasn't even getting many visitors at mass of late. Times had changed both for the neighborhood and for this once crowded but still glorious church. Father O'Gorman peered through the stained glass next to the heavy, mahogany entrance and could immediately see there was no danger, but there was certainly intrigue. A frail, old man with wispy, white hair was frantically pressing the buzzer and banging on the door as if the church was on fire.

The moment O'Gorman opened the door, the man dropped to his knees and pleaded for his confession to be heard in a church and inside a real confessional booth.

The old man was only 60 years old but had disguised himself to look as if he were in his mid-80s. His own mother wouldn't have recognized him; his teeth were almost green, and his hair was twisted and matted as if he hadn't bathed in a very long time and a razor hadn't touched his face in weeks. His hands were black with filth and his fingernails, gnarly and overgrown. Hair stuck out from his ears and nose, and his lips were chapped and infected.

O'Gorman helped the man to his feet and led him into the rectory. He was babbling about a moral conflict, an emergency to cleanse his soul of some horrible event in his life. O'Gorman, who had been a priest at St. Martin's parish since the 1950s, was retired but living "in residence" in the rectory. He had asked to spend his final days in the Bronx rather than in some lovely, bucolic home, where old priests were sent to wait for death. Father Edward's wish was granted by three different bishops and a cardinal because of their friendship with him and his many years of loyal service to the archdiocese. He had played the game very well within the Church and also had a few trump cards to use if his superiors suffered from sudden amnesia. O'Gorman knew where the figurative bodies were buried.

O'Gorman never wanted to be called monsignor and had no interest in climbing the career ladder, so his role as parish priest suited him just fine; he was happiest in familiar surroundings in a low key environment where he could behave as he pleased. When he turned 70, O'Gorman made a deal to stay on for a few more years before going into retirement. In the meantime, he'd stay in the same rectory where he had lived since he was a 28-year-old priest on his second assignment out of the seminary. He had spent only a few months at St. Anne's Parish in the South Bronx before he was moved quickly to St. Martin's. Now, he was 83 years old and spoke fluent Spanish. He had picked it up when the neighborhood became mostly Hispanic and African American in the early 1960s. He enjoyed long walks in the nearby Bronx Zoo and Botanical Gardens. His life was simple, but by the grace of God, it was exactly where he wanted it to be. His once tall and blond, good looks, marred only by a toothy smile, were long gone. The old priest was stoop-shouldered and bald with heavy, dark circles around his now dull, blue eyes.

O'Gorman was in mufti when the old man appeared at the rectory door, begging for a priest to save his soul from the fires of hell. Reluctantly, O'Gorman agreed to hear his confession. Father O'Gorman was alone in the rectory that night as there was a basketball game at St. Raymond High School in nearby Parkchester for the finals in the annual Christian Brothers tournament. The other parish priest, Father Vincent Ortiz, had gone to root for the legendary Ravens. Two of the team members had attended St. Martin's and would soon be getting athletic scholarships for college, a source of great pride for the school and parish. Both of those young men knew Father Edward very well. In fact, they knew him too well.

The archdiocese had decided to close St. Martin's school this year, and it was evident this was perhaps the last hurrah for any of the school's alum to reach for the brass ring through basketball. Sports was one of the few ways that students could escape from the poverty and danger of the area. The other ways out were death, prison, and the military. O'Gorman knew his days in residence were numbered, and he was patiently preparing for the inevitable. Sooner or later, God's waiting room in Orange County, New York or the nursing home, St. Patrick's, in the Bronx was in his destiny. What good would living in this rectory be anyway without the students, especially the boys, coming in and out of the church and residence?

O'Gorman fumbled for the key to the church's side door that hung on the kitchen wall as the old man continued to sob softly. O'Gorman threw the long-sleeved, white, linen surplice over his civilian attire and draped a purple stole around his neck so that it hung evenly just below his knees. He led him to the side of the church, and the old man shuffled beside him. They arrived just near an old grotto with the statue of Our Lady of Fatima looking down upon them. The grotto had been a popular place for First Holy Communion photographs for decades, but it hadn't had water flowing from it for over twenty years. The pump had failed, and there was no money to repair it, a sign of the times in a neighborhood where storefront churches and Santeria had taken their toll on the donations made to St. Martin. The second collection at Sunday masses had been stopped long ago as the baskets always came back empty.

Once inside, the electronic candles, which had long ago replaced the wax ones, and one security light, gave off just enough illumination for the two men to see their way to the back of the church and to the confessional that had Father Edward O'Gorman's name printed on a small, faded, bronze plaque on the light brown door.

Father Edward took the two ends of the purple stole into his hands and gently kissed the embroidered, gold crosses on each end. He then pointed for the old man to open the door to the compartment, where he would use the diagonal kneeler. O'Gorman opened the door to the priest's compartment and sat in the uncomfortable office chair that he had been using since the '50s. Creature comforts were few and far between. The confessional at St. Martin of Tours Church had the aroma of Pine Sol disinfectant and liquor. The Pine Sol was from the mop used by the once every two weeks porter that the archdiocese sent to clean up the church with a lick and a promise. The booze was emanating from Father O'Gorman. He slowly slid open the lattice.

"Bless me, Father, for I have sinned, it has been many years since my last confession."

"Go on, my son," O'Gorman responded into the pitch-black darkness, suppressing a belch from the two frankfurters and beans he had had for supper that evening.

"I have done many bad things, Father. I am sorry for what I have done and want to be forgiven so I can die and go to heaven. I killed many, many men during the war. I have not been to mass in 36 years. I have renounced my religion and my belief in Jesus Christ, our Lord."

"Let's start with the killings, my son. In service to your country during wartime, there is no sin in taking lives.

You did your duty as so many men did during World War II, and God fully understands that you were doing what you had to do for the good of many." Father Edward had consoled many men who killed in war.

"It was Nicaragua, Father, that damned Nicaragua, and I enjoyed the killing of those spics. I loved feeling their lives come out of them when I choked and stabbed them to death. Shooting them was not as much fun, but I loved that too, Father." The old man's voice had become clearer and seemed younger.

"You seem a bit too old for Nicaragua. Are you sure about this?" There was concern in Father Edward's voice.

"Oh, I'm sure of it, Father. You may remember the Deegan family from back in the day here at St. Martin's, Father. A good, Irish family with a bunch of wee kids. Do you recall the name, Father...Deegan?" the old man said with a perfect Irish brogue.

"Now, see here! What is the meaning of this? Is this your idea of a joke? Get out of my church this instant," O'Gorman said as he tried to open the compartment door to get back to the safety of the rectory. It was to no avail.

"Sorry, Padre, you can't leave just yet. The door is locked, and it's just me and you over here." The accent was now Bronx Italian ruffian.

"What the... who are you? What do you want?" Father O'Gorman was shaking like a leaf.

"Just a few questions is all, Father." The voice was that of a little boy. "What? What questions? My God, what do you want with me?"

"Answer the question, Father. The Deegans, do you recall the name?"

Again in the Irish brogue.

"I do... yes, I do. They moved away many years ago," the priest said, his voice quivering.

"Ah, yes, indeed, they did, and you followed them, now didn't ya? Ya followed them so that you could help save their souls from the devil himself, now didn't ya, good Father Edward O'Gorman. Yer own people. And they had that wee boy, John, don't ya remember? Ya insisted on calling him Sean, his true, Gaelic name, remember that, Father? They were from Donegal, don't ya recall?"

"Hail, Mary, full of grace, the Lord is with thee, blessed art thou among women, and bless..."

"Shut the fuck up, Edward. Just shut your fucking mouth," the old man screamed at the praying priest, who felt a trickle of piss run down his leg.

"I didn't do anything to that boy. I would never do such a thing. It wasn't me, I... I would never."

"That's what you all say. 'I would never, could never, the Lord as my witness, yada yada.' Well, Father, it's me, John Deegan. I've come to give you a bit of the unholy terror that you left with me since 1958, when I was a first grader. I'm going to do it slowly so that I can enjoy it and you'll remember it for eternity." Deegan used his own voice this time, punching the words slowly. "I've been watching your comings and goings for weeks, waiting for the right moment when you were all alone." Deegan paused for a long 10 seconds.

"Now say the prayer after me! Father. You know, the one you taught me over and over and over, but let's say the revised, politically correct, Vatican-approved version, Father... C'mon...here we go...

> "O, my God,
> I am heartily sorry for having offended Thee, and I detest all my sins,
>   because I dread the loss of heaven
>   and the pains of hell but most of all, because
>   they offend Thee, my God, Who art all good and deserving of all my love.
>   I firmly resolve,
>   with the help of Thy grace, to confess my sins,
>   to do penance,
>   and to amend my life.
>   Amen."

O'Gorman mumbled the prayer, but his heart rate had risen to the point where he was light headed and confused.

Deegan slowly opened the compartment where he was kneeling just inches away from the pedophile priest.

"Help... someone, help! For the love of God, please, someone help me." The priest was screaming, but of course, no one could hear him.

Deegan slowly removed the block that he had wedged into the wooden confessional door then turned the knob. The priest was now sobbing and begging for both help and forgiveness.

Deegan laughed in the voice of a small boy as he opened the door.

"Father Edward, remember you used to tell me… 'This is what God's love feels like.' Well… feel this, Father."

Chapter 2

The ancestors of the Deegan family had first set foot in the States so long ago the date had been forgotten. What was left of the family lore were words that were familiar to nearly every Irish family, the potato blight, wet rot, the *drochshaol*, or bad times, coffin ships, and the great hunger.

The present day Deegans knew they had lost relatives in the famine. This was not surprising as one in five of the Irish population died from malnutrition, disease, or violence. They heard from their grandparents that the Irish were punished for "the sins of the people," a superstitious, more than religious saying that caught on like the airborne fungus itself. The Roman Catholic Church did little to allay the fears of the faithful. The great, unwashed masses were never told that they were not being punished by the one, true, and benevolent God in heaven, that the blight was actually a phenomenon of nature, and that there was plenty of food the English kept from them. The stranglehold the Church had around the necks of the Irish people came with them on the coffin ships and has lingered and flourished since 1845.

John Joseph Deegan was the second born of six children to Jack Joseph Deegan and Maureen Duffy. He was the shining apple of his parents' eyes. In his mother's heart, soul, and mind, Johnny Boy was destined to be a priest from the day he was born. With John as a priest and by the grace of God, one of her daughters perhaps would join the convent. Maureen Deegan would have been happy to have closed her eyes and gone to heaven that very day. Her work on earth would have been complete as her children would work on saving souls and doing God's will to alleviate the sins of the people.

When John was three, his older sister, Margaret, would dress in white sheets and towels like the Dominican nuns and wear a rosary around her tiny waist, pretending to be teaching John his catechism lessons with a ruler in her hand to whack him on his knuckles or knees. Maureen and her friends would laugh at the sayings "Sister" Margaret would pass on to her baby brother, who remembered his lessons with uncanny recall.

By the time John got to first grade at St. Martin of Tours School, he could read, print his name and address, tie his shoes, and accomplish the one thing the nuns absolutely loved: he could recite the answers to the Baltimore Catechism questions verbatim.

Question: Who is God?

Answer: God is the Creator of heaven and earth and of all things. Question: What is man?

Answer: Man is a creature composed of body and soul and made to the image and likeness of God.

Question: Why did God make you?

Answer: God made me to know Him, to love Him, to serve Him in this world, and to be happy with Him forever in the next.

Question: Does God see us?

Answer: God sees us and watches over us. Question: What is Confession?

Answer: Confession is the telling of our sins to a duly authorized priest for the purpose of obtaining forgiveness.

From the day he started school in September 1958, John was destined to be a priest and climb the ladder of the archdiocese all the way to receiving his red hat from the pope. When his mother spoke to him alone, she referred to him as John Cardinal Deegan with a smile that the angels themselves would envy.

A photographic memory and ridiculously good looks were gifts John was given to do the Lord's work here on earth. His blond hair and piercing, blue eyes made him the Mickey Mantlesque, all-American poster boy, who would win the hearts of millions all in due time. His mother knew it, his siblings accepted it as fact, and the nuns believed it. Throughout his first year of school, there was never a mark less than an A or a 100%. His papers and report cards had more red and gold stars than the rest of the entire first grade put together. He was brilliant, perfect, and gorgeous, and he was a genius. He would also wet the bed until he was almost fourteen years old.

Chapter 3

Father Vincent Ortiz returned from watching the St. Raymond Ravens beat Rice High School in the basketball tournament at around midnight. The young priest enjoyed the crowd and liked seeing familiar faces and of course, rubbing elbows with the powerful Monsignor Joseph Barry, who ran the richest parish in the Bronx along with the largest Catholic cemetery in the country. St. Raymond Elementary and High School had been a powerhouse not only in sports but also in the political world of the archdiocese for decades. From the late 1800s, the twin domes of St. Raymond's Church had stood sentinel on East Tremont and Castle Hill Avenues as a beacon for the predominantly Irish, Italian, and German immigrants. The elite, financial status was a monument to the hard work and religious dedication of these people. Father Vincent was in awe of this church and its history. It was where he wanted to wind up working one day. Unlike O'Gorman, Vincent was a career climber.

The exposure this particular evening could garner would be beneficial to his career, especially if the new archbishop decided to close St. Martin's Church down completely. The rumors were already flying around that the archdiocese planned to close the underperforming schools and churches. St. Martin's school was first, so the church could not be too far behind. The logic fueled the gossip mill, and the likelihood that Father Vincent would soon be a free agent was real.

After the basketball game, Father Vincent took the two former St. Martin student ball players out for a celebratory pizza at Ronnie's Pizza on East Tremont Avenue. When they'd had their fill of the great pizza and Coca Cola, Father Vincent drove them back to the neighborhood. He said a silent prayer that they would go directly home as he advised rather than remain out too late and in harm's way. He felt badly about not inviting Father Edward to join in the festivities, but the boys were not overly enthusiastic about the older priest's presence. Ortiz didn't press the issue. He noticed the boys became quiet and almost sullen when he mentioned the old priest's name but didn't pursue the awkward moment. After all, it was their night and just as well as the game ended in overtime after 10 o'clock. Father O'Gorman was usually in bed by 10 anyway.

When the young priest entered the rectory, the place was dark except for the dim light that was barely visible from under the closed door of Father O'Gorman's bedroom. Father Vincent knew that the elder priest usually fell asleep while reading and so he made his way quietly to his own bedroom. He had an early mass to say the next morning and fell fast asleep.

***

Mrs. Nelly Santiago arrived every day at the rectory at 6:30 in the morning. She always prepared breakfast and lunch for the two priests. Their personal wash, ironing, vestment preparation, and house cleaning were all her responsibilities, and she worked for minimum wage, tithing 20% of her wages back to the Church. For Nelly, this was a labor of love for her Church and for her devotion to the Blessed Virgin Mary. By 2 o'clock in the afternoon, Nelly would be walking back to her small but immaculately clean apartment, where she had lived since 1968. That year, she had arrived in New York from *Bayamon*, located in the mountains of central Puerto Rico. Nelly worked at St. Martin of Tours from that day forward and at 64, had no plans to retire. The Church was her life. Her English was practically nonexistent for a person who had lived in New York City for 44 years, but her lovely and caring manner made the language barrier part of her charm rather than an impediment.

When she opened the door of the rectory the morning after John Deegan made his visit to Father O'Gorman, Nelly felt a chill go down her spine. The only other time in her life she had felt that haunting sensation was when her sister had called from Puerto Rico many years ago to tell her that their mother had died suddenly in her sleep.

At the entrance to the rectory, Nelly blessed herself, shrugged off the odd feeling, and headed for the kitchen to begin her day's work. As she recited her morning rosary, Nelly busied herself preparing hot oatmeal, toast, and coffee for the two priests.

Generally, Father O'Gorman would be roaming around the small living quarters, sitting in the study watching the morning news, or reading from one of his leather bound scripture books. Nelly found it odd that he was nowhere in sight, even though it was a Saturday. She went about her chores, awaiting the priests.

"*Buenos Dias,* Nelly, and how are you this beautiful day?" Father Vincent said as he entered the kitchen and made a beeline for the coffee pot. Nelly's *Cafe Bustello* was strong and aromatic just like the coffee Father Ortiz's dear mother made when he was at home.

"Buenos Dias, Padre, el señor nos ha dado un día hermoso."

"Yes, indeed. He has given us a beautiful day and wonderful coffee. I hope one day you will be able to greet me in English, my dear Nelly......

louisromanoauthor.com

www.ingramcontent.com/pod-product-compliance
Lightning Source LLC
LaVergne TN
LVHW021812060526
838201LV00058B/3340